So Geographers, in Afric-maps,
With savage-pictures fill their gaps;
And o'er unhabitable downs
Place elephants for want of towns.

JONATHAN SWIFT

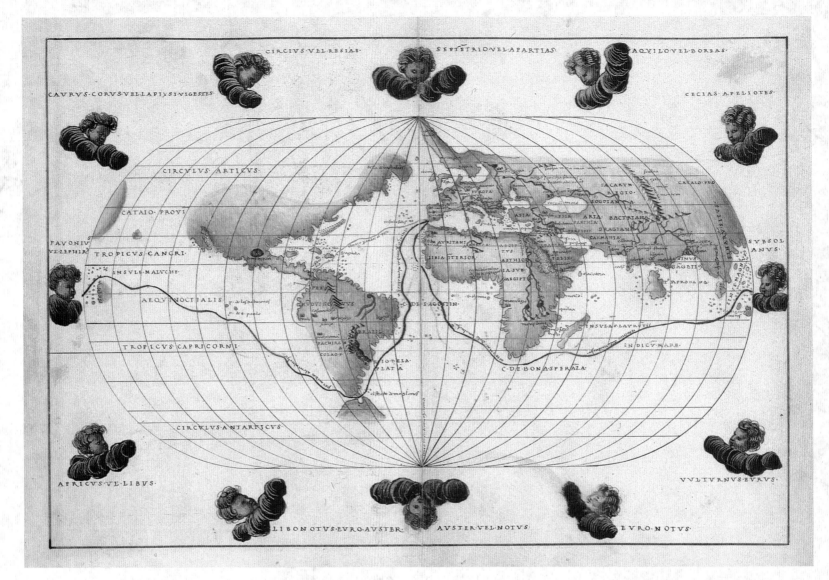

Venetian mapmaker Battista Agnese created this world map around 1544. The twelve cherub heads stand for the twelve winds, and each has a name on the map. The black line, which is actually silver turned black with age, shows the route that Portuguese explorer Ferdinand Magellan took on his voyage around the world. The gold line shows a route from Spain to Peru.

Mapping a Changing World

by Yvette La Pierre

Edited by Nancy Kober

Thomasson-Grant & Lickle
New York • Charlottesville

Baptista Boazio, an Italian artist who worked in London, made this map in 1589. Here the fleet of the English navigator Sir Francis Drake is attacking the Spanish settlement at St. Augustine, Florida. At the top center of the map is the Spanish fort. At the top left, some of Drake's men are raiding the town, which they captured and burned. The strange fish at the bottom left is supposed to be a dolphin.

TABLE OF CONTENTS

LIST OF ILLUSTRATIONS 6

INTRODUCTION: Mirrors of the World 9

CHAPTER ONE: Maps of Sticks and Stones 13

CHAPTER TWO: A Logical World 17

CHAPTER THREE: A World of Faith and Fancy 23

CHAPTER FOUR: Maps of Silk and Paper 29

CHAPTER FIVE: The Eve of Discovery 35

HOW TO MAKE THE EARTH FLAT 41

CHAPTER SIX: Mapping a New World 45

CHAPTER SEVEN: The Golden Age of Mapmaking 51

CHAPTER EIGHT: Mapping America 57

CHAPTER NINE: The Mythical Continent That Really Was 63

CHAPTER TEN: Our Changing World 69

CHAPTER ELEVEN: Pictures from Space 75

ILLUSTRATIONS

World map by Battista Agnese, around 1544..... 2

Plan of Drake's attack on St. Augustine by
Baptista Boazio, 1589 4

Map of the North Pacific by Antonia Zatta,
1776.. 7

Africa by Willem Blaeu, 1662 8

Satellite image of ozone over Antarctica,
1991 10

Map of the Crown Prince Islands by
Silas Sandgreen, 1925–26.......................... 11

Babylonian world map on clay tablet,
around 500 B.C. 12

Egyptian papyrus from the Fayum region,
around 330 B.C. 14

Stick chart from the Marshall Islands............... 15

World map from Claudius Ptolemy's
Geographia, 1482 16

The world according to Homer 18

The world according to Democritus................. 19

The world according to Eratosthenes
and Strabo 20

Greek coin map, fourth century B.C. 21

The Psalter world map, thirteenth century,
mapmaker unknown................................... 22

The world according to
Cosmas Indicopleustes, sixth century 24

T-O world map in the style of the
twelfth century 25

Creatures from Nuremberg Chronicle by
Hartman Schedel, 1497 .... 26, 27

Section of a map of the China coast by
Wan Li Hai Fang T'u, 1705 28

Chinese map, Jiangxi province,
eighteenth century 31

Woodcut plan of Nagasaki, artist
unknown, 1802 32

Cosmic being of the Jain religion,
eighteenth century 33

Sections of the Catalan Atlas by
Abraham Cresques, 1375............................ 34

1533 copy of a world map by al-Idrisi,
1154... 36

Road maps of France by Matthew Paris,
thirteenth century....................................... 37

Map of Africa with Prester John by
Diogo Homem, 1558 39

Political map of the world, Robinson
projection, February 1994 40

Comparisons of several common map
projections of the world 42, 43

The New World by Sebastian Münster,
1546... 44

Section of the Mendoza Codex,
Aztec book, sixteenth century 46

The village of Secoton, Virginia, by
Théodore de Bry, 1590............................... 47

Virginia by John White, 1585 48

Detail of beavers from map of North America
by Herman Moll, 1715 49

World map from Frederick de Wit's
De Zee Atlas, 1660 50

Copperplate engravers at work........................ 52

Ships and compasses by Matthäus Seutter,
from Atlas Novus, 1745 53

Detail from map of Virginia by Joshua Fry
and Peter Jefferson, 1755 54

Map of Iceland by Abraham Ortelius,
1585... 55

"Centennial American Republic and Railroad
Map" by Gaylord Watson, 1875................. 56

The "Duke's Plan" of New York,
mapmaker unknown, 1664.......................... 58

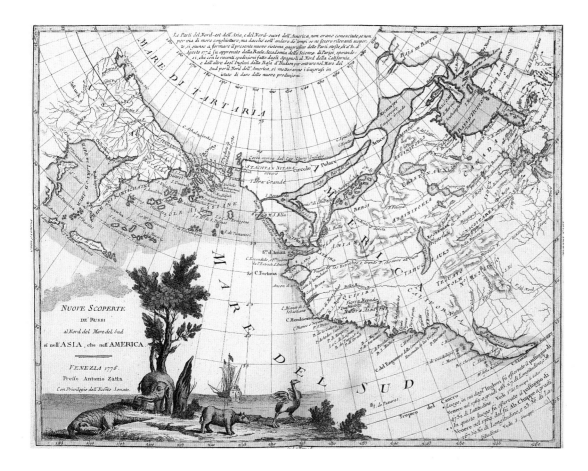

This map, made by Italian mapmaker Antonio Zatta in 1776, shows the northern region of the Pacific Ocean, where Alaska almost touches Russia. The animals that Zatta included—an alligator, elephant, rhinoceros, and ostrich—are African animals that would not really live in cold northern climates. The year Zatta made this map, the Revolutionary War broke out on the other side of North America.

Detail of surveyors from map of Kentucky by Luke Munsell, 1818......................59

"A Map of Lewis and Clark's Track" by Samuel Lewis (from a map by William Clark), 1814 60

1929 copy of a panoramic view of Los Angeles, 1871 61

World map by Abraham Ortelius, 1571 62

Detail from a survey of New Zealand by Captain James Cook, 1768 64

Map of Australia by John Rapkin, 1851 65

Satellite map of Antarctica, 1991 66

Five Dreamings by Michael Nelson Tjakamarra, 1984......................67

"The World at War" by the Army Special Service Division, 1943..................68

Eastern Europe before World War I 70

Eastern Europe after World War I 71

Eastern Europe in 1981......................72

Eastern Europe in 1994......................73

Earth from the Apollo 11 spacecraft, 1969 74

Radar image of volcano, Russia, 1994 76

Satellite image of flooding around St. Louis, 1993............................77

Computer-generated map of areas at risk for earthquakes, 1989......................78

Topographic map of Mount McKinley, 1982........................79

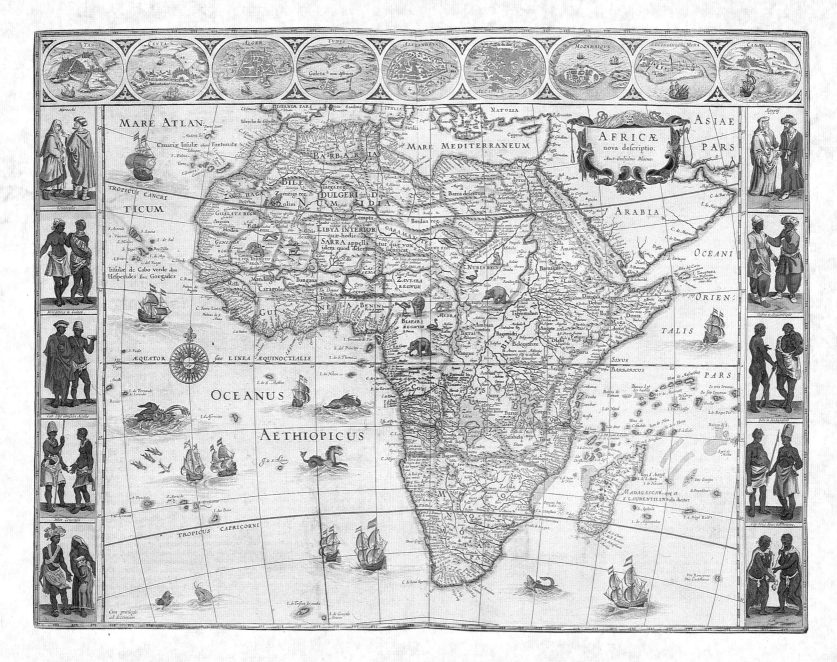

Willem Janszoon Blaeu, a famous Dutch mapmaker, made this map of Africa in 1662. Lions, elephants, monkeys, and other animals populate the continent, while Africans in colorful dress and bird's-eye views of African cities decorate the borders of the map. Europeans of this time had charted the coasts of Africa but had not yet explored its interior.

INTRODUCTION
MIRRORS OF THE WORLD

Do you know the way to Ear Island? It's the land where fishermen have ears so large that they cover their bodies. What about the island of Lixus, where a tree bears fruit of gold, or Milk Island, where milk comes from grapes?

You won't find these islands on a map today, but there was a time when maps were filled with strange places and outlandish creatures. Early mapmakers weren't trying to be silly. They were showing the world as they knew it, and some of their knowledge was based on stories, religious beliefs, and imagination.

For thousands of years, people have been drawing *maps*, pictures of their worlds on small, flat surfaces. Throughout history, maps have changed as people have learned more about the world through scientific discoveries, new inventions, and the voyages of great explorers.

Today, maps are more accurate pictures of the world, and we use them to find our way around, describe the special features of an area, and learn about places we may never visit. But

Ozone is a gas in the atmosphere that helps protect us from the sun's harmful rays. Some scientists are concerned because a hole has formed in the ozone layer over Antarctica. In 1991, the National Aeronautics and Space Administration took this satellite picture of the ozone over Antarctica. Blue colors show places where the ozone is low, and red areas mark higher, more normal ozone levels.

even now, maps continue to change as boundary lines between nations shift, as mapmakers develop new tools and new methods of showing the world on paper, and as scientists and modern-day explorers learn more about the world.

This book will take you on a journey around the world and through time, using some of the many marvelous maps of the world. Each chapter opens with an actual historical or modern map that you will explore to learn more about the world, the people who made and used the map, the events that shaped their lives, and the science of mapmaking. You'll begin by following some of the earliest maps through ancient worlds. You'll discover new continents as the explorers did and follow the mapping of the New World. Finally, you'll end up in the twentieth century and follow some of the events that have influenced the world map of today. You'll discover that maps do much more than tell us where we are, or what's over the next hill, or what lies across the oceans. Maps reflect how people live and think and what they know and believe. And just as ancient maps illustrate how people once viewed their world, modern maps are mirrors of our world.

Silas Sandgreen, an Eskimo hunter who had never seen a modern chart, made this map out of seal-skin and driftwood in 1925–26. It shows islands off the coast of Greenland. Yellow marks swampland, blue gray stands for lakes, black represents lichens, and the uncolored wood is the area covered by tides.

Babylonian world map on clay tablet, about 500 B.C.

CHAPTER 1
MAPS OF STICKS AND STONES

The object on the opposite page may look like a rock, but it is actually a map. And not just any map—it is the oldest surviving map of the world. Babylonians, an ancient people who lived in Mesopotamia, where Iraq is today, made the first surviving map of the world about twenty-five hundred years ago. They carved their view of the world on a small clay tablet scarcely bigger than your hand.

Look at the big circle etched on the bottom half of the stone. This suggests the Babylonians believed the world was like a flat disk. At the top of the circle is a curved line that symbolizes mountains. From the mountains, two lines run down the center of the circle. These are probably the Tigris and Euphrates Rivers.

The rectangle crossing the rivers is Babylon, the capital city. Other important cities are marked by small circles, though only one, Deri, is named. The mapmaker also used circles to represent regions: Armenia is above and to the right of Babylon, and Assyria is slightly below Armenia. Habban is to the left of Babylon.

The outer circle surrounding the entire world is the ocean. The Babylonians called it the Bitter River, probably because the sea is salty. Living beyond the circular ocean in the triangle-shaped islands were all sorts of imaginary beasts. Though most of the islands have been chipped or worn away, historians know from the writing on the top and back of the tablet that there were

This ancient Egyptian scroll was made around 330 B.C. from papyrus, an early kind of paper. This section is believed to show a real place, Lake Moeris, which once covered most of the Fayum region of northern Egypt but is now a desert. The half-human, half-animal figures are gods who have come to honor Sobk, the crocodile god, whose legendary home was in this region.

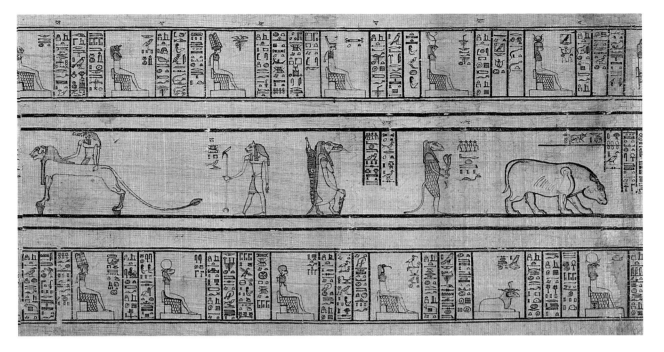

seven islands originally. The writing describes the different islands. For instance, the fourth island, the one in the top left-hand corner, is a place of light "brighter than that of sunset or stars," and the fifth island, to the right, is a place "where the sun is not seen."

Although this is the oldest map of the world that we know about, people had been making maps, and perhaps world maps, long before this. No one knows when or where the first person got the idea to draw a picture to show a location. But it is easy to guess why. People have always been curious about where they are and how to get to other places. And it's easier to draw a map than to explain in words where something is. In fact, mapmaking may have developed before written language, making it one of the oldest forms of communication.

The word "map" comes from Medieval Latin and originally meant cloth or napkin, a common material for maps in the Middle Ages. But since ancient times, people have made maps from whatever materials were on hand, including rock, wood, clay, marble, animal hides, silk, metal, and papyrus, a kind of paper made from a plant.

Beginning thousands of years ago, people carved and painted on rock walls and caves throughout the world. Rock art images include animals and people, as well as lines, circles, and other shapes that some believe may be maps.

Over time, people in different parts of the world developed their own ways of making maps. The ancient Egyptians drew real places on papyrus and painted maps to the afterlife in tombs. Eskimos carved maps of coastlines in wood and ivory, and native people in Siberia and North America drew maps on bark. The people of Mexico were very skilled at mapmaking, and European explorers often depended on their maps and guides. Before Europeans reached the South Pacific, the people of the Marshall Islands were making stick charts. They tied sticks together with fibers to show winds and wave patterns, then added shells or bits of coral to indicate islands.

Many ancient civilizations, including China, Greece, and Persia, now called Iran, became very skilled at making maps and developed the science of mapmaking, called *cartography*.

The Babylonian clay tablet appears to be just a fragment of a larger object that described the whole universe, including the heavens. You'll notice when you look at the tablet that Babylon is in the center of the world. Early mapmakers commonly put themselves in the center of the universe, just as we can be self-centered in our view of place today. If you were to describe the room that you are in now, you would probably locate the different items in the room as they relate to you. Perhaps there is a window to your right, a couch across the room, and a table next to you, on the left. Without thinking, you have placed yourself in the center of the room.

The Babylonian map of the world started other mapmaking traditions that continued for thousands of years, such as using symbols for mountains and cities and showing the world as a circle of land surrounded by water. Drawing strange creatures outside the bounds of the known world became the mapmaker's way of saying, "I don't know what's really out there."

The Babylonian map, and all the earliest maps, were the first attempts to answer questions that still fascinate people: Where am I? What lies beyond the edge of my world? Does anyone or anything live there?

Before Europeans explored the South Seas, the people of the Marshall Islands in the South Pacific made maps for sailing out of palm leaf fibers and shells. The curved sticks mark the directions of waves, and the tiny shells are islands. Only certain sailing masters knew how to make these maps, and the secret was handed down from father to son.

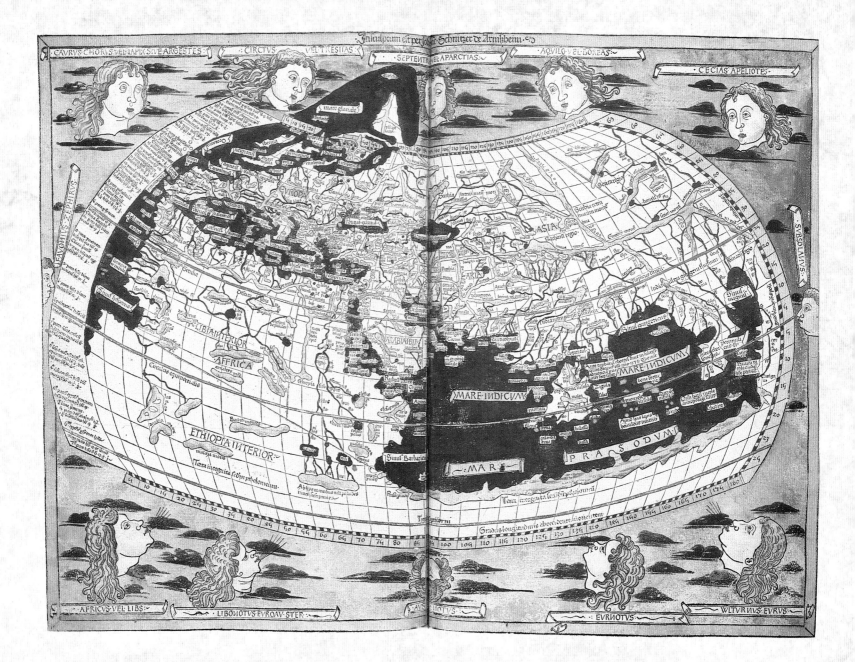

World map from Claudius Ptolemy's *Geographia*, 1482

CHAPTER 2
A LOGICAL WORLD

Around 2100 B.C., a great civilization began that, over the next three thousand years, would lay the foundations of modern science, including the science of mapmaking. Like the civilizations before them, the ancient Greeks (actually various groups of people we call the Greeks) were curious about the world around them. What is the true shape of the earth? How big is it? What parts of the world can people live in? Ancient Greek scholars used logic and science to try to understand the universe.

Claudius Ptolemy, who lived and worked in the second century A.D., was a scientist and astronomer in Alexandria, the center of learning in the Greek world. His work, such as this world map, brought together the ancient Greeks' achievements in mapmaking and influenced the development of modern cartography. In his book *Geographia*, Ptolemy gave instructions for drawing a round world on a flat surface, suggested how to divide the world into regional maps, and located some eight thousand places in the ancient world. No single work has had the impact on mapmaking that this book had. Ptolemy is called by many "the Father of Geography."

This map wasn't actually made by Ptolemy— no maps made by Ptolemy survive. It was printed much later, in 1482, in the German city of Ulm, based on information in *Geographia*, which did survive. Though Ptolemy had been dead for centuries, his ideas lived on.

This drawing from *Long's Classical Atlas*, an 1867 textbook on ancient geography, shows the world as it was known to Homer, the major Greek poet. Homer lived around the ninth century B.C. and wrote the long adventure poems called the *Iliad* and the *Odyssey*. Homer thought the world was a flat circle, surrounded by a great ocean (*Oceanus* on this map). Greece is outlined in pink in the center. Homer also knew about the Mediterranean Sea (*Pontus Pelagus*) and Northern Africa (*Libya*), including Egypt (*Aegyptus*).

If you compare Ptolemy's world map with the modern world map in the center of this book, it looks very odd. Ptolemy's world consisted of only three continents—Europe, Asia, and Africa. Actually, Ptolemy thought there was more to the world, but he believed in mapping only the parts of the world he knew to be habitable, places people had visited and measured.

All the continents on Ptolemy's map are misshapen, but Africa is the strangest—it doesn't really stretch that far south and then curl around to the right to connect with Asia. Apparently Ptolemy thought the Indian Ocean was landlocked and that it was impossible to sail around the bottom of Africa (although earlier the Egyptians had sent an expedition around Africa). This false notion discouraged early European sailors who wanted to sail down the west coast of Africa, around the continent, and east to Asia. Ptolemy and other early Greeks thought there must be a huge continent to the south of the Indian Ocean to balance all the weight of the continents up north. (The early Greeks liked their world to be orderly and symmetrical.) They called this continent *Terra Australis Incognita*, which means Unknown Southern Land. Explorers looked for it until the late 1700s.

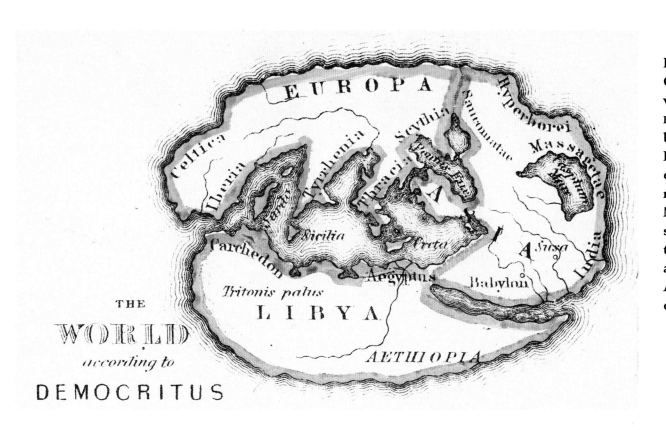

THE
WORLD
according to
DEMOCRITUS

Democritus was a Greek philosopher who lived around 400 B.C. This 1867 map is based on his writings. By the time of Democritus, Greeks knew more about Asia. Notice the inland sea—today called the Caspian Sea—at the far right of Asia, the continent outlined in blue.

Despite its strange look, Ptolemy's world map contains some ideas and mapmaking techniques that we still follow today. For instance, did you notice that the world looks curved on this map? That's because Ptolemy believed that the earth was round like a ball, or *spherical*. This was a revolutionary idea for the ancient Greeks, because people had long believed that the earth was flat. Some believed it was a flat disk floating on water or in the air. Others thought the flat world was supported by four elephants standing on a turtle's back.

Ptolemy did not come up with the idea of a round earth, and we're not certain who did. The Greek philosopher Aristotle was the first to provide evidence to support the theory. Aristotle, who lived in the fourth century B.C., noticed that during an eclipse the shadow of the earth on the moon was curved. That meant the earth must be spherical. In his book, Ptolemy included the ideas of many other Greek scholars, including Homer and Strabo.

Along the left margin of his map, where the Latin writing is, Ptolemy divided the world into zones, or areas, where people could and could not survive. These zones were based on distances

This drawing shows the world as it was known to the Greek thinkers Eratosthenes and Strabo. Eratosthenes, who lived around 200 B.C., calculated the distance around the earth. Strabo, who lived around A.D. 20, collected information about the world from Roman soldiers. This map covers more of Europe and Asia than the earlier Greek worlds. Notice England (*Brittania*) at the upper left, the Arabian peninsula (*Arabia*) near the lower center, and India near the lower right.

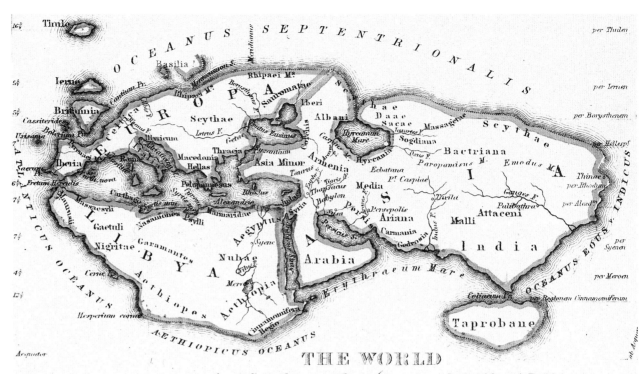

THE WORLD
according to Eratosthenes and Strabo (from about B.C. 200 to A.D. 20)

from the *equator*, the imaginary circle around the middle of the earth. (In the Ptolemy map, the equator is the thick orange line running through central Africa.) The Greeks thought that people could not live in the cold zones, farthest north and south of the equator, where the sun was low. Some also thought that the zone right around the equator, where the sun was directly overhead, was too hot for human life, but Ptolemy disagreed.

Puffing on Ptolemy's world from all directions are the twelve wind blowers, which were popular on maps as late as the eighteenth century.

On some maps, their expressions and the blasts of wind coming out of their mouths told readers something about the wind. The cold North Wind, for instance, often looked grouchy and had icicles in his beard, while the East Wind was a merry young boy blowing a gentle breeze.

Ptolemy adopted one of the most important mapmaking ideas to come out of the Greek world: the use of evenly spaced lines to describe the locations of features on a map. The lines that run east and west—from right to left—on Ptolemy's map are called lines of *latitude*. The others that go north and south—or top to bottom—are called lines of *longitude*. With this system, which we still use today, you can describe any place on the face of the earth as the point where its latitude and longitude intersect. Though Ptolemy was not the first to use the lines, he did come up with the names latitude and longitude. Ptolemy adopted another practice that all mapmakers now use: placing north at the top of the map and east at the right-hand side. Ptolemy also used symbols for mountains, rivers, and lakes, as mapmakers still do today.

You'll notice on Ptolemy's map that the lines of longitude and latitude are curved, as they are on many modern world maps. This was Ptolemy's answer to the problem of how to show, or *project,* a round world onto a flat surface. Ptolemy drew curved lines to give the sensation of looking at a round world.

For the most part, Ptolemy's world map was as accurate as it could be with the information available to him. But he did make the wrong choice about an important piece of information.

In the third century B.C., a librarian by the name of Eratosthenes calculated the distance around the widest part of the earth, called the *circumference,* using a shadow, a well, camels, and some simple mathematics. He came up with a figure amazingly close to the true circumference of 24,860 miles. A later scientist, however, decided he had a better method of calculating the circumference. He arrived at a figure of about 18,000 miles, and it was this smaller figure that Ptolemy accepted. This mistake, copied and recopied along with Ptolemy's world map for the next two thousand years, changed the course of history. It led Christopher Columbus, who owned and studied a Ptolemy world map, to believe he could easily sail from Europe west to Asia. Instead, he ran into America, a big continent that Ptolemy and the Europeans who came after him had not even known was there.

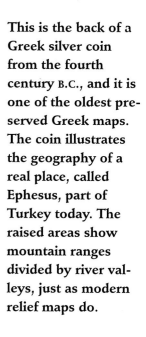

This is the back of a Greek silver coin from the fourth century B.C., and it is one of the oldest preserved Greek maps. The coin illustrates the geography of a real place, called Ephesus, part of Turkey today. The raised areas show mountain ranges divided by river valleys, just as modern relief maps do.

The Psalter world map, thirteenth century A.D. , mapmaker unknown

CHAPTER 3
A WORLD OF FAITH AND FANCY

World maps made in the Middle Ages, from about the fifth century to the fifteenth, are a blending of geography, religious history, and imagination. This map, called the Psalter map, is a little illustration from a thirteenth-century copy of the Book of Psalms. It can tell you what many medieval Europeans believed about both the physical and the spiritual worlds.

The Psalter map is one of the most beautiful of the medieval world maps, with its bright colors, fancy scrollwork, and fantastic illustrations. But it isn't—and wasn't meant to be—an accurate geographic picture of the world at the time.

You may be wondering what happened to Ptolemy's practical map, with its orderly lines and zones. Very few copies of the works of Ptolemy and other Greeks were available to Europeans. Not only were these works in a foreign language,

but they had to be written and drawn by hand, a very time-consuming task. In addition, the leaders of a new religion called Christianity weren't interested in the books and maps of the Greeks. Instead, they turned to the Bible to answer their questions about the world, and the world maps they made during this time were more religious than geographic. They were meant to teach people about Christianity, not show them how to get from one place to another.

At the top of the Psalter map, Christ, with an angel on either side, stands over the round world. Most Christian mapmakers believed the

The Christian monk Cosmas Indicopleustes drew a box-shaped view of the world in the sixth century. (This copy of his work was made in the eleventh century.) Cosmas was following the Bible, which said that the tent the prophet Moses lived in was a model for the whole world. Cosmas thought people lived in the bottom of the box and the lid held the heavens.

earth was round. But some mapmakers, who read in the Bible about the "four corners" of the world, reasoned that anything with four corners could not be round, and they drew rectangular worlds. In the sixth century, a monk named Cosmas Indicopleustes drew a map in which the world looked like a rectangular box or a trunk with a bulging lid to hold the heavens. Below, an enormous mountain rose out of the sea. According to Cosmas, the sun revolved around this mountain, causing day to turn to night.

More influential writers than Cosmas, such as Isidore of Seville, continued to draw the world

as round. Isidore's circular world maps of the sixth and seventh centuries became a popular model for medieval maps, including the Psalter map. In these maps, an ocean in the shape of an O surrounds the whole earth. Inside the O, the three known continents—Asia, Europe, and Africa—are divided by three bodies of water in the shape of a T. The upright pole of the T is the Mediterranean Sea. The Nile and the Don Rivers form the top of the T. European church leaders liked this orderly picture of the world, and T-O maps, as they became known in modern times, remained popular until the fifteenth century.

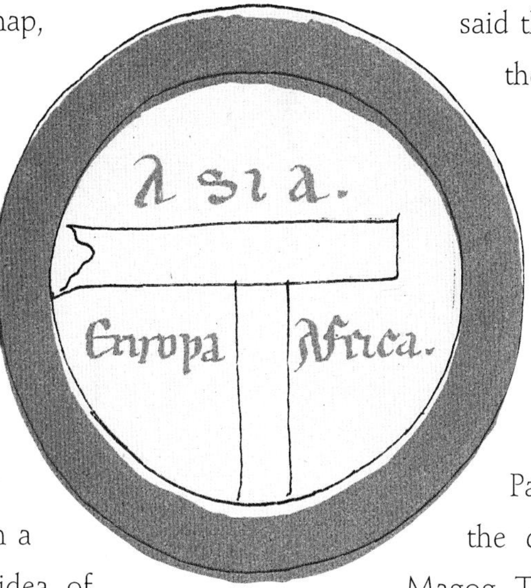

In the center of the Psalter map, in the red circle, is Jerusalem, the Holy City. From about the thirteenth to the fifteenth century, T-O maps almost always showed Jerusalem in the center of the Christian world. Nearly all medieval maps had east, or the Orient, at the top, which is why we say today that maps are "oriented" in a particular direction. To get an idea of how medieval Europeans saw the world, turn the map in the middle of this book to the left so that China is near the top.

Paradise, the Garden of Eden from the Bible, was an important feature on many medieval world maps. On the Psalter map, you'll find Paradise in the east at the top of the map in a black circle. Putting Paradise on maps encouraged people to go looking for it. An Irish monk named Saint Brendan set out across the Atlantic Ocean in search of Paradise in the sixth century. Legend has it that he and a crew of sixty men spent five years at sea and encountered many amazing things along the way, including an island of pure white birds who said they were fallen angels, a fire-breathing dragon, and the devil. At last they found a beautiful island with a holy man who

said that they had found the place they were looking for. The story of Saint Brendan's wondrous voyage spread throughout Europe, and Brendan's Paradise could be found on maps as late as the eighteenth century.

To the left, or north, of Paradise on the Psalter map lie the dreaded tribes of Gog and Magog. They are held back by a wall of iron, shown here as a half-circle with a gate in it. According to the Bible, the imprisoned hordes would someday break loose and wipe out the Christian world. Mapmakers often placed the land of Gog and Magog in the far north because they didn't know what really belonged there. Filling maps with monsters and marvelous lands was a common practice for early mapmakers, who quickly discovered that people were more likely to buy a decorated map than one with a lot of blank spaces.

The Bible wasn't the only source of information for medieval mapmakers. Strange beasts, such as those along the right-hand edge of the Psalter map, came from the works of early travel writers, including Pliny, Lucian, and Solinus.

Pliny the Elder was a first-century Roman

T-O world maps, popular in the Middle Ages, look like the letter T inside the letter O. The red circle, or O, is the ocean. Inside it are the three known continents of Asia, Europe, and Africa, divided by the Don and Nile Rivers (the top bar of the T) and the Mediterranean Sea (the stem of the T). Maps like these were meant to show the general order of the world, not the exact shape of the continents. In 1849, the Viscount of Santarém published a book with more than one hundred copies of maps from the Middle Ages, including this twelfth-century map.

Bizarre imaginary creatures from Roman travel writers found their way onto many maps of the Middle Ages. They included the dog-headed Cynocephali; the one-eyed Cyclopes; the Sciopods, who rested under the shadows of their enormous feet; and the headless Blemmyae, who had their faces on their chests. These examples come from the *Nuremberg Chronicle*, a late fifteenth-century book that drew upon earlier writers.

scholar whose book *Natural History* was considered *the* encyclopedia of natural wonders. And wonderful they were. Among the imaginary people and places of Pliny's world were the inhabitants of Ear Island off the coast of Germany. This tribe of fishermen had ears so large they could hear fish under the sea. In the desert of Africa lived a group of people who were headless but had eyes and a mouth in their chests. Look for them on the Psalter map.

Lucian of Samosata described Pumpkin Island, where pirates sailed in boats carved from giant pumpkins, and the island of Cork, where people with cork feet walked on water.

The most famous travel writer was Gaius Julius Solinus, a Roman scholar of the third century. He told a good tale but was known as "Pliny's Ape" because he took much of his information from Pliny. He wrote about dog-headed men, glow-in-the-dark birds, and the umbrella men of India who each had a single leg with a foot so big that the man could rest under the shade of it. He told of an animal in Germany that looked like a mule but had such a long upper lip that the only way it could eat grass was to walk backward. In Africa there were hyenas so frightening that just their shadow could scare the bark out of a dog, and a tribe of people who each had four eyes.

Many of these fanciful creatures reappeared in a book called the *Nuremberg Chronicle*, first printed in 1493. In fact, they showed up on maps and in books as late as the eighteenth century.

Some of the fantastic creatures Solinus described were not made up. He wrote that the people of Britain were covered by "flesh embroidery." As odd as this may sound, what he was actually describing were people covered with tattoos. Because most medieval Europeans had seen so little of the world, they had no way of sorting the fact from the fiction.

Section of a map of the China coast by Wan Li Hai Fang T'u, 1705

CHAPTER 4
MAPS OF SILK AND PAPER

T he Chinese, founders of one of the oldest civilizations in the world, began making precise maps more than two thousand years ago. During the Middle Ages, the Chinese were producing accurate maps of their kingdom, as well as such faraway

places as India, the Nile River, and part of the Mediterranean Sea.

Chinese maps, such as this one of the China coast made by a man named Wan Li Hai Fang T'u in 1705, were generally very practical. The map is a bird's-eye view of the coast from Qingdao in the north to Canton in the south (north is to the left). You are seeing only a small segment, though, because the whole map is fifty-one feet long. It was drawn on paper and folded like an accordion into an album. The map was probably used for military purposes—the small flags, squares, and circles you see mark forts, naval stations, and other defense sites.

The Chinese were more concerned with mapping the things they could see—coastlines, cities, roads—than those they couldn't, such as unknown lands. Chinese rulers knew that they could govern and defend their empires better if they had accurate maps with detailed information.

The oldest surviving Chinese maps were made of silk and sealed in a tomb in the Hunan province in 168 B.C., where they were discovered in 1973. They are more detailed and accurate than most ancient maps. The mapmakers used symbols to show villages and provinces, rivers and roads, mountain ranges, and military forts. Wavy lines, for example, symbolized mountains, thin lines were roads, and thicker lines showed the size and flow of rivers.

Early Chinese mapmakers thought the world was square and that most of it was taken up by their own country. By about 400 B.C., however, new religions with different ideas about the shape of the earth were reaching China from India. Maps from Buddhism and other religions showed the world as a disc surrounded by the ocean with India and Mount Meru, a sacred place, in the center of the world. China occupied only a small portion of the earth. Though early Chinese mapmakers preferred their precise, rectangular maps, a few Chinese maps do show the influence of India's disc-shaped world and surrounding ocean.

Very few geographical maps from ancient India survive, but there are many wonderful images of the earth and universe based on Indian beliefs about the creation of the world. Some show the world as a tortoise—the shell, head, and feet represent different areas of the earth. In one Buddhist map, the world is a floating lotus blossom. In some maps made by followers of the Jain religion, the universe is shaped like a human body. Like medieval European world maps, these maps were meant to be more religious than practical.

By the end of the third century B.C., the Chinese were producing the most accurate maps in the world, in part because they used a grid—a system of evenly spaced lines covering the map—to help measure distances and locate features on the map. According to one story about the invention of the grid, the emperor asked a young woman to paint a map for him. She said she would rather embroider him a map with silk thread, whose colors lasted longer than paint. As she embroidered, she realized that it was easier to locate cities and roads on the map if she used the vertical and horizontal threads in the silk, called warp and weft, as a grid.

The Chinese advanced mapmaking again when they invented paper from bark, rags, and other fibers at the end of the second century B.C. They made multiple copies of maps by first carving the image in stone, then placing a piece of paper on top and rubbing the paper with chalk to transfer the image to the paper.

But perhaps China's greatest contribution to cartography was the use of a magnetic needle for steering a ship, or navigating.

Centuries ago, people discovered that a special kind of iron ore called magnetite or lodestone could make a needle act strangely. If you rubbed a needle with magnetite, then floated it in a cup of water, the needle always pointed north, no matter which way the cup was turned. Today we know that this happens because the earth's magnetic poles attract the metal. But in those

This Chinese map comes from an eighteenth-century atlas of the Jiangxi province. It shows green rivers, blue mountains, and yellow land with forts and villages.

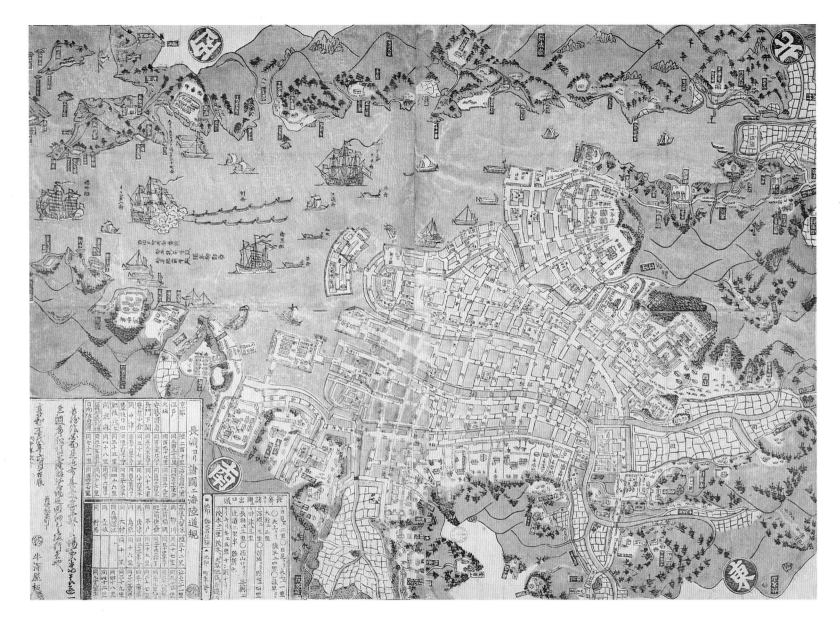

This Japanese woodcut, made in 1802 by an unknown artist, shows Nagasaki, an important town for trade between Europe and Japan until the Japanese expelled the Christians in 1640. Only the Dutch were allowed to continue trading, but they had to stay on the island of Deshima, the slightly curved shape just left of center with the tiny Dutch flag. Among the ships in the harbor are two Dutch merchant ships—one firing a salute—and, to the far left, a Chinese junk.

days, magnetite was mysterious and frightening. Some people thought that magnetite was magic and could cure all sorts of illnesses. Others told of magnetic islands that could pull the nails out of a passing ship.

The Chinese were the first to use a magnetic needle for navigating by sea, sometime around the eleventh century A.D., and by the early 1400s they were using it on ambitious voyages across the Indian Ocean and the China Sea. Under the famous Chinese navigator Cheng Ho, the Chinese sailed all the way to India, Arabia, and East Africa. It would be many years before Europeans would attempt such voyages.

In 1405, on the first of seven voyages, Cheng Ho set sail with sixty-two ships loaded with gold and other treasures. The map of Cheng Ho's last voyage is the oldest surviving Chinese sea chart and includes information from his earlier voyages.

Cheng Ho and his crew weren't on a mission to conquer new lands. They simply wanted to show the rest of the world the greatness of their kingdom and impress them with their gifts. In 1433, a new emperor decided that the expeditions were expensive and unnecessary. So for many years thereafter, the Chinese stayed put.

And that ended the great age of exploration for China. Other countries, however, were just getting ready to discover the world.

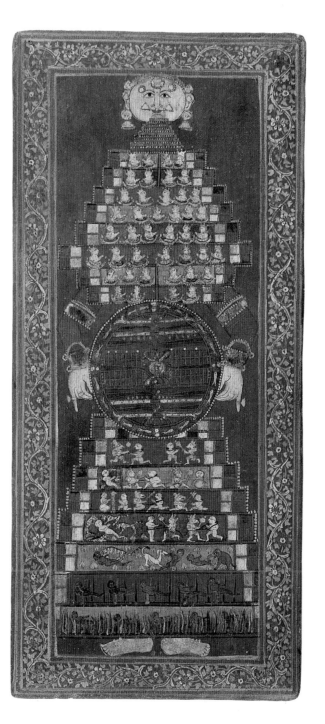

This painting, which resembles a person's body, appears on the cover of an eighteenth-century book made in India. Followers of the Jain religion of India drew maps like this to explain their beliefs about the creation of the world and the connection between human life and the universe. The circle in the middle of the body stands for the earth. Above are the eight levels of heaven, with the head at the top. Below, in the skirt, are the seven levels of hell.

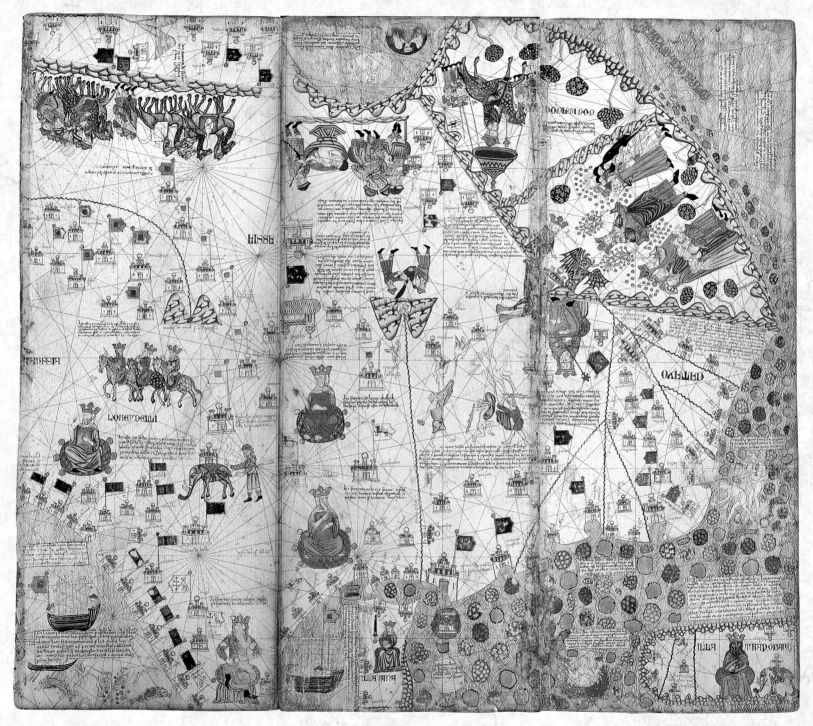

Sections of the *Catalan Atlas* by Abraham Cresques, 1375

CHAPTER 5
THE EVE OF DISCOVERY

It is one thing to travel on land following a map full of mistakes, but for a ship's captain, an accurate map is a matter of life and death. Around A.D. 1300, navigators developed sea charts, also called *portolan charts*. Unlike the Psalter map and other medieval world maps, sea charts were full of practical information, such as descriptions of coasts and harbors and the location of dangerous rocks underwater. This world map from the *Catalan Atlas* includes information from sea charts, as well as from the sailors who used them.

A man named Abraham Cresques made the *Catalan Atlas* in 1375, most likely as a gift for the King of France. It illustrates the tempting riches of the East—both true and mythical—that helped persuade medieval Europeans to explore more of the world.

Kings and palaces, cities and ships, and caravans of camels in rich colors and gold cover the panels of the atlas. The three panels you see here show Asia. Cresques also illustrated several amazing legends, such as the pearl divers in the Indian Ocean, who were protected from sharks as if by magic. Look for them at the bottom of the first panel.

The lines criss-crossing the map are called *rhumb lines*, and they represent the various directions of winds. (Navigators identified as many as thirty-two wind directions.) Sailors laid their courses along these lines. The points at which many lines come together are called *wind roses*.

Al-Idrisi, a famous Arab cartographer, made a map like this for King Roger of Sicily in 1154. (This copy was made in 1533.) South is at the top of this map. If you turn the map upside down, you can find Europe on the upper left, Asia on the upper right, and Africa stretching across the bottom. Unlike Ptolemy, al-Idrisi left the Indian Ocean open and did not connect Africa to Asia. The large mountain shape with lines coming out of it marks the place where al-Idrisi thought the Nile River began.

Around the same time that portolan charts were invented, someone got the idea to fasten a magnetic needle to a card with a picture of a wind rose on it, making an instrument called a *compass*. When allowed to swing freely, the needle always pointed north. By placing the compass over a wind rose on a sea chart, a sailor could determine his direction, then follow the corresponding rhumb line across the map to chart his course. Because of the compass, sea charts had north at the top, not east like the medieval world maps.

Using compasses and sea charts to explore, sailors brought back new information about the shape of coastlines. Abraham Cresques used this information to make the *Catalan Atlas* one of the most accurate maps of its time. The shores of Northern Europe are more defined than in earlier maps, and for the first time India and China are close to their proper shapes.

The *Catalan Atlas* included information provided by Arab sailors and mapmakers, some of whom had studied the books of Ptolemy and other Greeks and made corrections to them. During their conquests and extensive trade missions, Arabs journeyed east to Asia, west into Europe, and south to the Sahara Desert. Trade may even have taken Arabs as far north as Lapland, near the North Pole. One great Arab traveler journeyed south to the equator and saw that, contrary to what many ancient Greeks had believed, people were indeed living there.

The most famous Arab cartographer was a man named al-Idrisi. He was born in North Africa about 1100, and started traveling when he was sixteen. He traveled through North Africa, much of Europe, and the Near East. Eventually he put his personal experience to work for the King of Sicily producing accurate maps and a guide for travelers. He corrected some of Ptolemy's errors, making clear, for example, that Africa was not connected to Asia and that the Indian Ocean was open. Al-Idrisi is especially important because he passed information from the Arab world to Europeans.

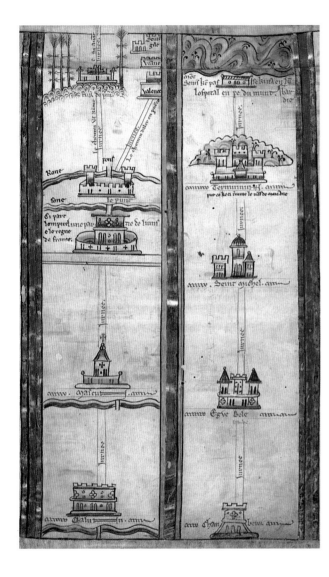

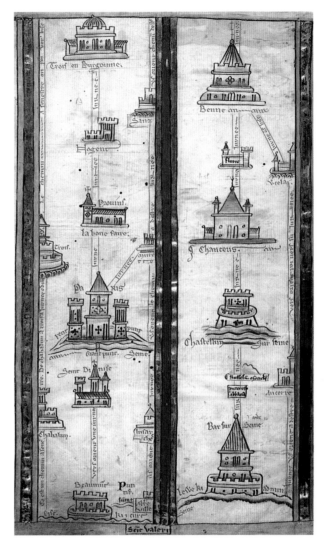

Medieval road maps were laid out in straight lines, or strips, and used by merchants and pilgrims traveling as far as the Holy Land. The English monk and historian Matthew Paris drew this map, the earliest known English road map, in the 1200s. These four sections show two routes through France of about thirty miles each. The sketches show churches and other stopping points, and the red lines show the travel time in days.

Europeans also did some traveling during the Middle Ages, though they didn't go as far as the Arabs. Many Christians made special trips to Jerusalem, their Holy City, even though it was controlled by Muslims after the seventh century. Muslims, followers of the prophet Mohammed, began making the journey dangerous for Christians in the eleventh century.

This conflict prompted Christian Europeans to try to take back Jerusalem from the "unbelievers." They began a series of nine wars, called the Crusades, that lasted from 1095 to 1271. Hundreds of thousands of European men, women, and children marched toward the Holy Land, armed with guidebooks, maps, and crosses. They saw lands they had only imagined, met people from faraway places, and discovered new foods, such as lemons, apricots, and melons. Though the Christians weren't successful in taking Jerusalem, the Crusades changed their lives forever.

During the First Crusades, rumors reached Europe of a great Christian king in the East called Presbyter John, better known as Prester John. He was said to possess untold wealth and power and would help the Christians win the Crusades—if only they could find him. European kings sent men in search of Prester John after he supposedly wrote a letter describing his kingdom: "Honey flows in our land, and milk everywhere abounds. In one of our territories no poison can do harm and no noisy frog croaks, no scorpions are there, and no serpents creep through the grass." Prester John and his enchanting kingdom popped up in various places on maps for hundreds of years.

Europeans never did find Prester John, but as they traveled about looking for him, they brought back stories of real riches in distant lands. Europeans also read with amazement the account of Marco Polo, a man from Venice who traveled to China with his father and uncle when he was seventeen and served in the court of the great ruler Kublai Khan. Marco Polo described the splendor and wealth of exotic places like Tibet, Japan, Sumatra, and Ceylon, and his reports found their way onto the *Catalan Atlas*, the oldest surviving map to show his travels. You can see the Polos on the map at the beginning of this chapter. They're pictured on horseback near the top of the left panel.

Other missionaries and merchants brought back stories of gems, spices, and silks that were abundant in Asian countries, known as the Indies. In the last panel of the *Catalan Atlas* shown here, islands rich in cinnamon, nutmeg, cloves, and other spices, which Europeans valued as highly as gold, fill the sea off the coast of China. Although most of these islands were imaginary, they helped fuel a frenzy of exploration among Europeans eager to have these new trade goods and riches.

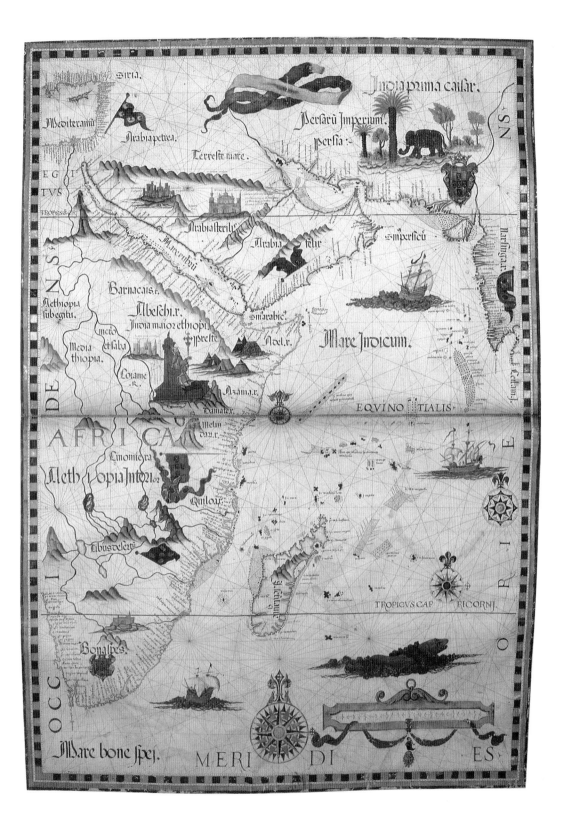

This map from Diogo Homem's 1558 atlas shows the mythical Christian king Prester John sitting on his throne in Eastern Africa, where Ethiopia is today. Prester John's kingdom was originally thought to be in Asia, but after explorers found no trace of him there, mapmakers moved him to Africa. (As for Diogo Homem, he fled his home in Portugal after killing a man in a fight in a rough section of Lisbon where the mapmakers mingled.)

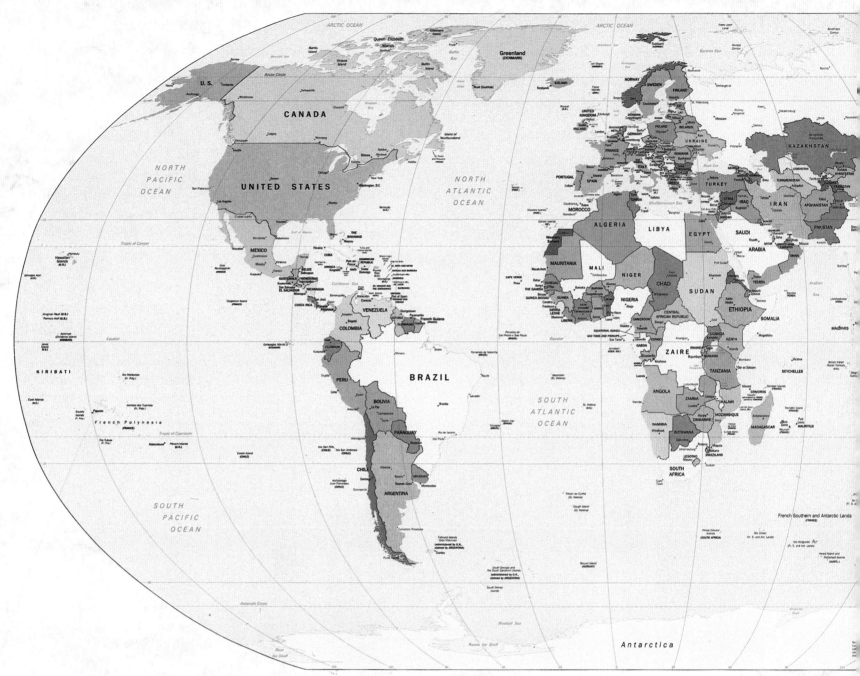

Political map of the world, Robinson projection, February 1994

How to Make the Earth Flat

It's easy to put a round world on a round globe. Putting a round world on a flat surface is another story. If you tried to press a whole orange peel flat on a table, you'd get a pretty good idea of the problem mapmakers face when they try to draw the world on a flat piece of paper. It's impossible to do without either cutting the peel or twisting and pulling the peel out of shape, which is called distortion.

All flat maps, then, are distorted to some degree. The amount, location, and type of distortion depends on how the mapmaker drew, or projected, the rounded sections of the globe onto the flat surface. Since the days of Ptolemy, map *projections* have come in almost every imaginable shape, including a rectangle, a circle, a star, and a heart. Some map projections preserve the correct sizes of continents but stretch them out of shape. Others keep shapes true but distort sizes. To minimize distortions, mapmakers may slice the globe into sections or cut it into flowerlike petals so that it will lie flat.

Because no projection is perfect, cartographers look for the one that best suits the purpose of the map. That's what Gerardus Mercator did in 1569 when he realized that navigators needed

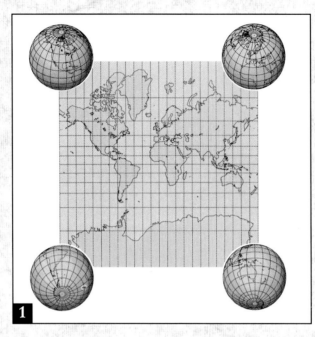

1

(1) This form of projecting the world onto a flat page is named after Gerardus Mercator, the famous Flemish geographer who created it. It is one of the most common projections. The Mercator projection is useful if you are steering a ship, but it is not a good choice for an all-purpose map because it distorts, or twists, the sizes and shapes of continents. The four drawings of globes in the corners of this illustration use an Orthographic projection, which shows how the continents look on a real globe but can only reveal half the world at a time. See how different Greenland looks on the flat Mercator projection and on the globe drawing in the upper right.

maps they could easily steer by. Because the earth is curved, following a straight line on a flat map didn't take navigators where they wanted to go. Mercator drew the earth so that a straight line on his map would take you the same place a curved line on a globe would, which allowed navigators to plot their courses as straight, not curved, lines. In order to do this, he had to stretch the world quite a bit. But the areas in the center of the globe on either side of the equator, where explorers did most of their sailing, were distorted the least. As a result, land masses near the poles were stretched way out of shape so that they appeared much larger than they really were. On the Mercator projection, Alaska looks as big as Brazil, although it is

less than one-fifth the size, and Greenland looks seventeen times bigger than it really is.

Many different types of projections, including *equal area projections*, have been tried since the sixteenth century to address the problems of the Mercator projection. In these maps, there is no distortion in the sizes of any continents, but the continents are stretched out of shape. To keep continents from looking large at the poles, as in the Mercator projection, equal-area projections stretch the world vertically, making land south of the equator look longer than it really is.

The map on the preceding page uses the Robinson projection, which is a compromise between the Mercator projection and equal-area projections. This kind of map has become popular recently. It has some distortion of the size of the continents, but their shapes are more realistic.

The important thing to remember is that all flat maps distort reality. Even the practice of always putting north at the top of maps influences the way we perceive the world. Try turning the map on the previous page upside down, and you'll see the world in a whole new way.

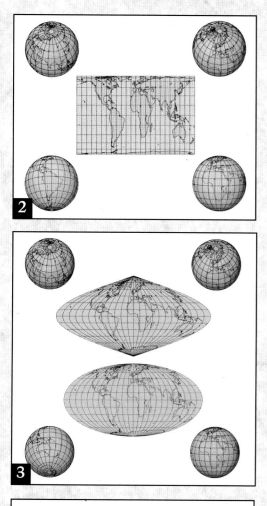

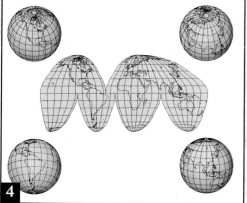

(2) The Gall-Peters projection, which is used in this map, is an equal-area projection. This means that the sizes of the continents are correct. On this map, Africa looks larger than North America—which it really is. The shapes of the continents are still somewhat distorted in this projection, which makes the land in the south seem longer and the land in the far north seem wider than on a globe. Notice how long and narrow Africa looks compared with its shape on the globe drawing in the lower right.

(3) These two oval-shaped projections of the world are called Sinusoidal (top) and Mollweide (bottom) projections. In the Sinusoidal projection, the continents are close to their proper shapes in the center of the map, but are squeezed together near the North and South Poles. In the Mollweide projection, the continents are stretched a little in the center, but are less crowded around the poles. See how crowded Russia appears on these maps, especially the top one, compared with its shape on the globe in the upper left.

(4) This map uses the Interrupted Goode Homolosine projection. This projection slices the world into sections, like a flattened orange peel. The continents keep almost the same shapes as on the globes.

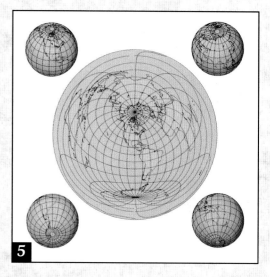

(5) This map is made with the Azimuthal-Equidistant projection, and its center is in the midwestern United States near Chicago. Mapmakers can center this projection on any point, such as your hometown. In the middle of the map, distances and directions are accurate, but at the outer edges, shapes and sizes are greatly distorted. This projection is sometimes used to show flight distances for airplanes. Can you find Australia on this map?

The New World by Sebastian Münster, 1546

CHAPTER 6
MAPPING A NEW WORLD

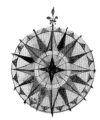

Do you recognize North and South America on this map? Though not fully formed yet, the continent is beginning to take shape. Sebastian Münster, a German cartographer, made this map and first published it in 1540, fewer than fifty years after Columbus stepped onto the continent then unknown to Europeans.

The map, which was a best-seller in its day, was a big improvement over earlier maps. For the first time, North and South America are connected to each other but not to Asia. Even so, for the next twenty-five years, some mapmakers would continue to connect America and Asia. Christopher Columbus had been even more confused—he was convinced that America *was* Asia until the day he died.

When Columbus set sail in 1492, in search of a more direct route to the spices of China than sailing around the tip of Africa, he knew all there was to be known about the world in his day, including the fact that the earth was round.

In the early 1400s, an old copy of Ptolemy's book *Geographia* resurfaced. The book contained instructions on how to make a map of the world. It was translated into Latin, the language of European scholars. Thanks to the development of printing around the same time, many copies of this book were produced, and scholars across Europe read it. By the time of Columbus's travels, Ptolemy was once again the geographical authority.

The Mendoza Codex is a sixteenth-century book made by the Aztec Indians, who lived in Mexico. This section, which has maplike features, shows the founding of the Aztec capital of Tenochtitlán, today Mexico City. According to legend, an Aztec priest told his people to build a city where the sun, shown here as an eagle, landed on a cactus with prickly pears shaped like human hearts.

According to Ptolemy and other maps and globes that Columbus studied, the distance from Spain to the Indies was only about five thousand miles, with several small islands spaced like stepping stones along the way. We now know it's closer to fourteen thousand miles, and those small Atlantic islands were just inventions of mapmakers. Columbus got a little nervous when he didn't find some of the small islands that were on his map, but when he came across land four thousand miles from Spain, he figured he must have reached the islands of eastern Asia. Actually, he had landed on Guanahani in the Bahamas, which he renamed San Salvador. Columbus had stumbled across an entire continent that the Europeans did not know about.

Soon after, in 1494, Spain and Portugal signed the Treaty of Tordesillas, which drew an imaginary line west of the Cape Verde Islands. Everything to the east belonged to Portugal, everything west to Spain. The two flags, one next to *Hispaniola* and one at the extreme right of the Münster map, under *Sinus Atlanticus*, indicate the two sides. No one argued that the land rightfully belonged to the people who were already living there. In fact, one of the first things Columbus did when he landed in South America was to gather the native people, who did not understand his language and had no idea what was going on, to stand as witnesses as he claimed the land for the King and Queen of Spain.

Europeans made maps of the New World and changed Native American names to European names. One of the few native names to survive is Cuba, shown on Münster's map. Ironically, Europeans often called on native people to help them make maps of the lands they were claiming for European nations. Native Americans, particularly the Mixtec people of Mexico, made beautiful maps of their cities and lands.

After Columbus, many explorers came to the New World, driven by the search for a direct water route from Europe west to the Indies. One of these explorers, Amerigo Vespucci, claimed that it was he, not Columbus, who first set foot in the New World. Many believed him, and the mapmaker Martin Waldseemüller decided to pay tribute to Amerigo by naming this new continent after him in his 1507 map of the world. Waldseemüller eventually changed his mind and took the name "America" off later maps, but the original map was so popular that the name stuck.

The Münster map celebrates the first trip around the world with a large picture of Ferdinand Magellan's ship *Victoria*. In 1519, Magellan left Spain with five ships and 265 men. Only one ship, *Victoria*, and 18 men returned, but Magellan was not one of them. He was killed in a fight with Philippine natives a year earlier.

Magellan thought it would be a short trip from South America to the Indies, but his trip proved the globe to be as big as Eratosthenes had said. Along the way he explored the coast of Brazil and found a winding passage at the bottom of South America where a ship could pass from the Atlantic Ocean to the Pacific. Münster labeled the strait *Fretum Magaliani*, after Magellan.

Théodore de Bry, a Flemish engraver who worked in Germany, based his illustrations for *Americae*, published in 1590, on the drawings of John White, whose own map is shown on the next page. This engraving of the Indian village of Secoton, Virginia, shows native crops, including corn, sunflowers, beans, and squash.

In 1524, the Italian navigator Giovanni da Verrazano, while exploring the eastern coast of America, reported seeing a large body of water, which he believed nearly divided North America in two and led to China. This false Sea of Verrazano, which splits the continent between *Terra florida* and *Francisca* on Münster's map, persisted for more than one hundred years and convinced Europeans that there was a direct water passage to the Indies. Myths like this one

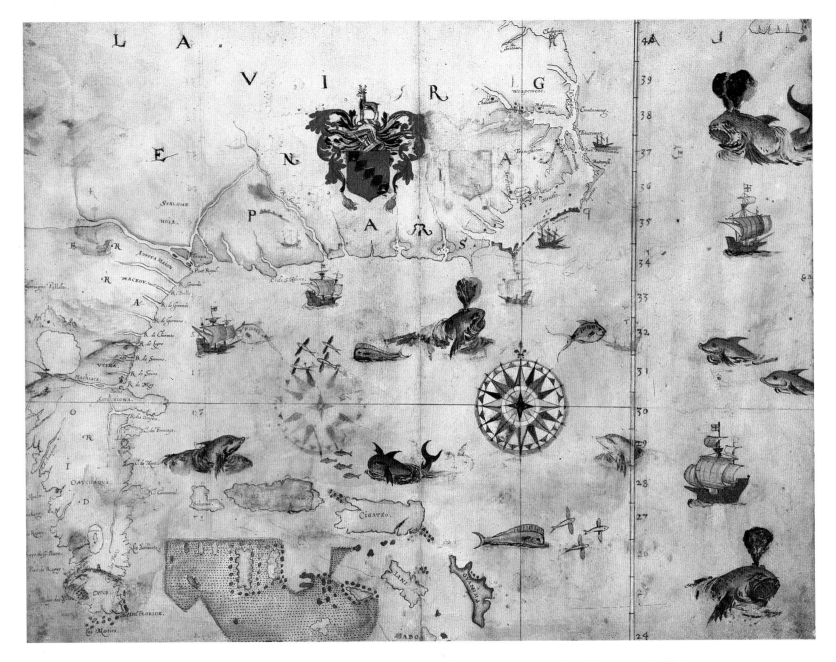

John White, one of the first English settlers of America, drew this map in 1585. The upper half shows the coast of what was then called Virginia but is now North Carolina. The long thin islands off the coast are the Outer Banks. Between them and the mainland is Roanoke Island, where John White's party started an unsuccessful settlement. The red dots mark French forts and Native American villages. The map also pictures whales, flying fish, dolphins, and other sea life that White found in the New World.

were partly responsible for the settlement of North America, which Europeans hoped to use as a jumping-off point to the riches of the East.

In the late 1500s, England tried settling North America. The first English colony, at Roanoke Island off the coast of what is now North Carolina, failed. In 1587, more than one hundred English women, men, and children tried to start another colony at Roanoke Island, under the leadership of John White, who had been in the first group. White sailed back to England to establish better supply lines. By the time he returned in 1590, nothing was left of the second Lost Colony. Among those who disappeared was his little granddaughter, Virginia Dare, the first English baby born in the New World. To this day, no one knows exactly what happened to the settlers.

White, a watercolorist, painted the people, animals, and plants of the area and made the first map of the region, then called Virginia, in 1585. Most cartographers, however, had never been to the New World, so they relied on secondhand reports to fill their maps. The drawing of cannibals on the right-hand edge of South America in Münster's map indicates what he had heard about the people who lived there.

Other mapmakers used their imaginations. That's why in many early maps of America, sea monsters and dragons appear alongside deer and

London engraver Herman Moll placed this fanciful scene of hardworking beavers on his 1715 map of the British settlements in North America. Niagara Falls is in the background. On the map, Moll wrote that beavers work "with great order and wonderfull Dexterity."

bears, alligators swim in Lake Superior, and beavers appear larger than grizzly bears. Europeans were fascinated by accounts of the hardworking American beaver. In one scene, copied and recopied on maps of North America, beavers walk erect, carry sticks in their paws, and work in humanlike assembly lines.

Studying many of these early maps, Europeans must have thought North America was inhabited almost entirely by fur-bearing animals like deer, bear, beaver, muskrat, fox, and a few bison that looked like tame cows. Maps of the continent emphasized its natural resources and helped make the New World look more attractive to settlers.

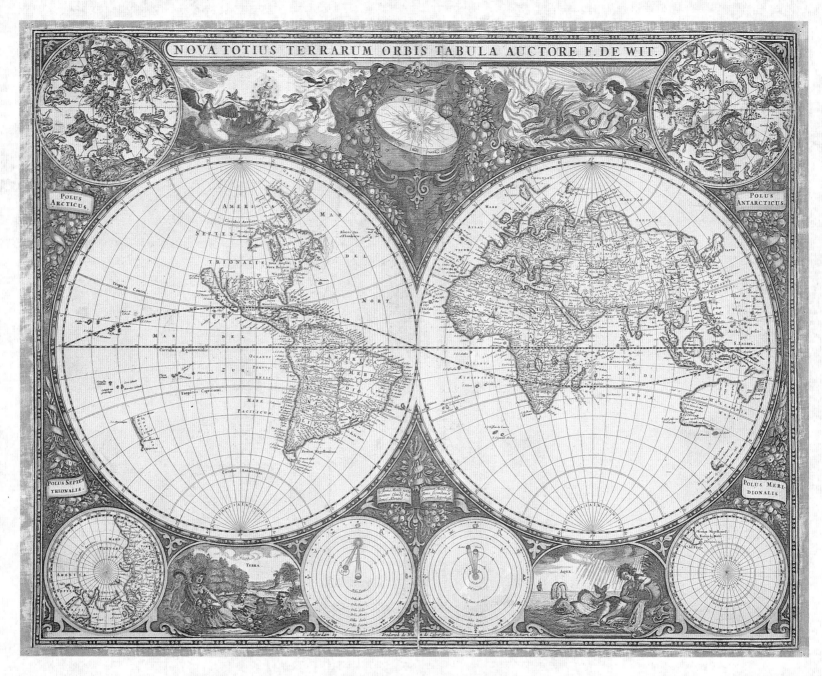

World map from Frederick de Wit's *De Zee Atlas*, 1660

CHAPTER 7

THE GOLDEN AGE OF MAPMAKING

After the discoveries of Columbus and other explorers, maps became all the rage in Europe. Adventurers, kings, and armchair travelers were intrigued by the new lands and curious about what else might be found over the horizon.

Mapmakers were only too happy to indulge this new passion. And the time was right for a mapmaking craze in the sixteenth and seventeenth centuries—the art of printing was improving, and explorers continued to feed mapmakers new information. Mapmaking became big business.

As you might guess from looking at this ornate map of the world, published in 1660, many maps were made for rich people. Large, fancy maps decorated the halls of royal palaces and were featured in grand public shows and at parties. Many people framed and hung maps instead of paintings in their homes, and mapmakers spent a great deal of time and energy turning maps into artistic masterpieces.

In the middle of the sixteenth century, the Dutch became the leading mapmakers. Amsterdam was a center of trade, so mapmakers could get firsthand information from sea captains from all over the world. This was also the age of the great Dutch painters, and many artists worked for Holland's important map publishers.

The Dutch were also masters at copperplate engraving, which had replaced woodcutting in northern Europe as the best way to print maps. With woodcuts, printers drew the design on a

In this illustration, seventeenth-century engravers are hard at work in their studio, preparing metal plates and making paper copies. The man on the right is feeding an inked plate topped with paper through the press.

block of wood, then cut away the background so that the design stood out from the wood. Then the printer spread the block with ink and pressed paper against it, leaving a copy of the design on the paper. With the new technology, the engraver cut the design into a copperplate and spread ink over the surface and into the grooves of the cut design. Then the engraver wiped the extra ink from the surface of the plate so that ink remained only in the grooves. The printer then placed a piece of paper on top of the plate and ran it through a press. The press squeezed the paper very tightly against the plate until the ink transferred from the grooves of the plate to the paper, creating a print. Mapmakers liked to work with the soft copperplates because they were easier to add to and correct.

The mapmaking industry was organized into groups of workers, or guilds. Each guild was responsible for a different step of producing a map. For example, some men painted decorations on title pages and borders of maps, while others made sea charts. The head of each guild supervised the workers to make sure that all work met high standards.

This was also the age of the *atlas*, a collection of maps bound into a single volume. Ortelius and Mercator, two of the most famous men in mapmaking history, each came up with this idea at about the same time. When Abraham Ortelius was a young man, his father died. In order to make more money to support the family, Ortelius began to buy maps. His sisters mounted them on linen, then Ortelius colored them and sold them at fairs. Before long, he had a thriving business and traveled all over buying and selling maps.

Ortelius had a customer, named Aegidius Hooftman, who had a large collection of maps. Hooftman complained that some of his maps were too big and bulky, while others were so small he got a headache trying to read the fine print. Hooftman dreamed of a collection of good maps, each on a single sheet of paper the same size, bound in a book that could be neatly stored on a bookshelf. Ortelius made his dream come true, and the book of maps was so popular with Hooftman and others that Ortelius decided to make a book of the best maps of every country.

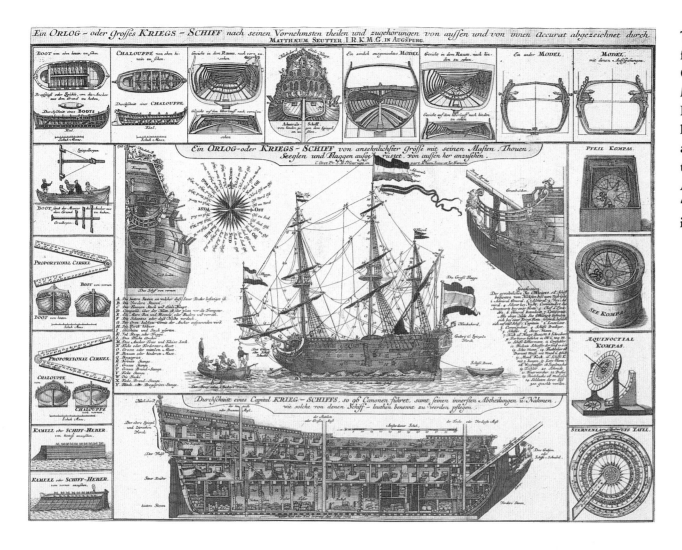

This illustration comes from a 1745 atlas by German mapmaker Matthäus Seutter. It depicts the various kinds of sailing ships and compasses used to navigate the seas. At the bottom is a "cutaway" view of the inside of a large ship.

It took ten years to locate and engrave the maps, but in 1570 Ortelius published *Theatrum Orbis Terrarum*, the first modern atlas. The "Theater of the World" was such a success that a second printing was needed within three months.

In 1578, Ortelius's friend and fellow mapmaker, Gerardus Mercator, began planning his own grand collection, which would include up to one hundred maps. Unfortunately, he didn't live to see the publication of the complete edition. Mercator's collection is especially important because it used the word "atlas" for the first time. He also corrected many common mistakes that had been on maps for centuries. Mercator is best

This *cartouche*, or title picture, comes from a 1755 edition of a map of Virginia and its neighboring colonies made by Joshua Fry and Peter Jefferson, the father of President Thomas Jefferson. It shows a typical wharf scene with plantation owners and slaves preparing tobacco for shipment to England. Cartouches often pictured the people, dress, and life of the places shown on the map.

known, however, for his method of projecting the round world onto paper, which is still used today.

Less than a hundred years later, Frederick de Wit published the large map at the beginning of this chapter as part of his *De Zee Atlas*. De Wit, a Dutchman, was one of the most famous map engravers of the late 1600s. His work was known for its beauty and accuracy. De Wit decorated the border of this map, which shows the earth in two halves, or *hemispheres*, with many pictures, including illustrations of the four elements that people believed were essential for life—air, water, fire, and earth. Air is symbolized in the upper left by the woman sitting on a cloud with eagles. Fire rides a chariot drawn by dragons near the sun, opposite Air. At the bottom of the map, Earth lounges with a lamb and a lion, and Water pours liquid from a jug under stormy skies.

Mapmakers like de Wit knew that colored maps sold better, so they colored their engraved maps by hand. Many artists used standard colors in their maps, such as blue for seas, green for forests, and red for towns. In the borders and

cartouches, they were free to use more colors and elaborate illustrations. The cartouche contains the map's title, the mapmaker's name, and other information about the map. The cartouche at the top of the de Wit map is fairly plain, but some were very large and complicated, with pictures of cherubs, Greek gods, ships, plants, animals, or local people worked into the design. Mapmakers often placed the cartouche in an area of the map that they knew nothing about and otherwise would have left blank.

To make their maps more eye-catching, mapmakers continued to decorate them with pictures of sea monsters, people, and beasts. But as explorers made more discoveries, mapmakers needed more room on their maps for the facts. Slowly, fancy cartouches and illustrations moved off the maps and into the borders only.

Even without fantastic creatures, these maps still contained plenty of fantastic ideas. In the de Wit map, for example, California is shown as an island, a notion that would appear on some maps until the early eighteenth century.

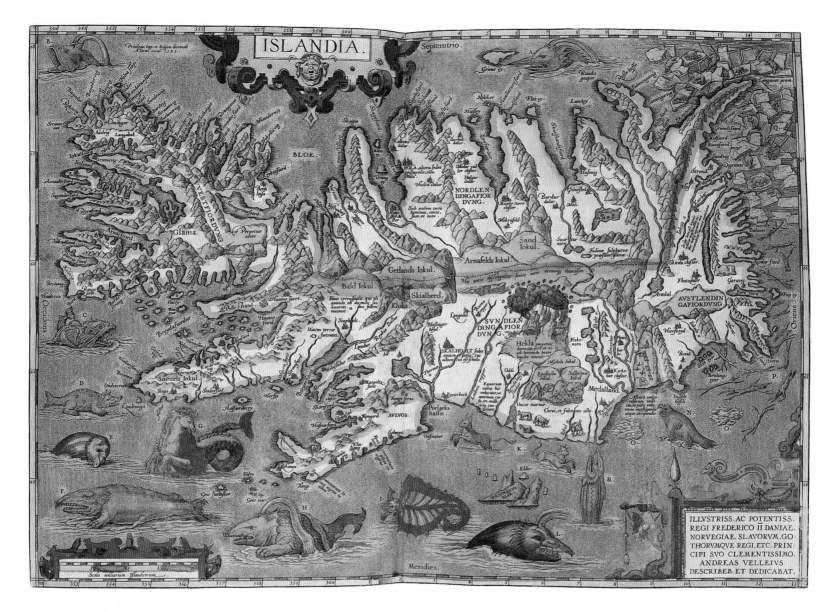

In this 1585 map of Iceland, Abraham Ortelius not only filled the sea with monsters, but he also labeled them and described them on the back of the map. Ortelius wrote that the creature labeled M "hath bene seene to stand a whole day together upright upon his taile . . . and greedily seeketh after man's flesh." Ortelius also included real animals—the bears fishing from icebergs in the upper right.

"Centennial American Republic and Railroad Map" by Gaylord Watson, 1875

CHAPTER 8
MAPPING AMERICA

When the United States won its independence in 1776, Americans knew surprisingly little about their continent. By the new nation's centennial, one hundred years later, the country had been mapped from coast to coast.

In that relatively short period, Americans had gained a complete picture of their country, thanks to surveyors, railroads, new mapmaking techniques, and the heroic deeds of many explorers. This railroad map, made especially for the centennial, is decorated with pictures of Independence Hall, the U.S. Capitol, and the Centennial Exhibition in Philadelphia, seen at the top of the map. The map even contains the text of the Declaration of Independence.

Of course, the mapping of America did not begin at independence. George Washington, whose familiar face appears on the Centennial Map, was a colonial *surveyor* before he became the first president. A surveyor is someone who goes out into the field to take measurements and gather information cartographers need to make maps. In 1745, when he was thirteen years old, George Washington found some of his father's surveying instruments and set to work near his home. One of his first contributions to mapmaking was "A Plan of Major Law. Washington's Turnip Field as Survey'd by me." Washington had to give up surveying when he became a general in the American Revolution, but he remained interested in mapmaking all his life.

The English ships in the harbor suggest that this map of New Amsterdam, now New York City, was drawn shortly after the Dutch surrendered this settlement to the British in 1664. Known as the "Duke's Plan," this map shows the Hudson River, "Longe Isleland," and several New Amsterdam landmarks, including the Governour's Garden, the Governour's House, a Dutch fort, and, near the top left, Passage Place, where the ferry left for Brooklyn.

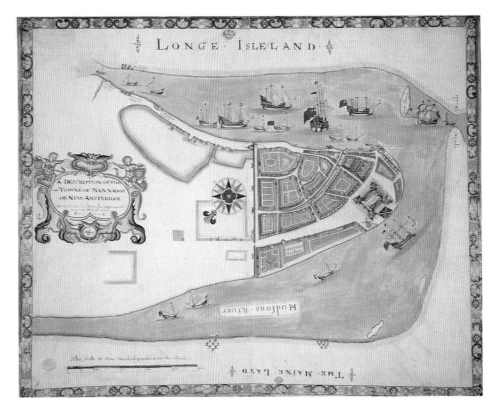

quickly selling land west of Pittsburgh, Pennsylvania, then the door to the frontier. Government leaders decided that the easiest way to do that would be to divide the land into rectangles of equal size and sell them to the public. Hutchins, and surveyors after him, divided the West into townships of six square miles each, containing thirty-six sections of 640 acres.

After winning independence, the former colonists were free to plan—and map—their future. Surveyors headed into the frontier to map boundaries for new states, towns, and roads. And they made a good living in the process. Frontier surveyors were paid in money or shares of land. Daniel Boone, a legendary pioneer, got half of all the new lands he surveyed in Kentucky.

In 1785, a geographer named Thomas Hutchins began a different type of survey that would shape the look of the entire American West. The government wanted to make money by

When you fly over the Midwest or look at a map of the United States, you can clearly see the checkerboard result of these surveys. In the West, unlike the East, roads, fields, and even states, particularly in the "four corners" region of Utah, Colorado, New Mexico, and Arizona, form neat squares and rectangles.

In the 1860s, the Civil War briefly interrupted the mapping of America's West, though mapping continued in the East and South, where battles were likely to be fought. Following the war, existing cities grew rapidly and new ones sprang up in newly settled territory. Maps of cities became popular, particularly those showing a *panoramic* or bird's-eye view of a city.

Railroad companies published maps, like the Centennial Map, showing the network of rail lines criss-crossing the country. These maps often included scenic views, lists of train stations, and distances between cities. Railroad companies passed out these maps, which were often printed in different languages, to new immigrants to encourage people to settle along their rail lines.

As more people began to ride trains in the mid-1800s, the demand for maps skyrocketed. Mapmakers took advantage of new printing techniques that allowed them to make maps and corrections more quickly and cheaply. As a result, more and more people had maps of the country. These maps, and the ability to get to new territories by railroad, helped spur settlement westward. Settlers and gold seekers believed that to the west lay lands of great riches.

None of this expansion would have been possible, however, if explorers hadn't first paved the way. The first great American explorers were Meriwether Lewis and William Clark.

In 1803, when the United States bought an area called Louisiana from France for $15 million, the nation more than doubled in size. The new land included the present states of Arkansas, Iowa,

This detail from Luke Munsell's 1818 map of Kentucky pictures a group of surveyors at work. This was the first official map of Kentucky and was based on information collected by Kentucky surveyors.

Missouri, and Nebraska, and parts of Louisiana, Minnesota, Oklahoma, Kansas, Colorado, Wyoming, Montana, and North and South Dakota. Little was known about these mysterious new lands, so President Thomas Jefferson sent Lewis and Clark out to explore.

Lewis and Clark left St. Louis on May 14, 1803, following the course of the Missouri River. Their goals were to find a land route, and perhaps a water route, all the way to the Pacific and to learn as much as they could along the way. One and a half years later, Clark stood where the Columbia River empties into the Pacific, in what is now Oregon. He chose a tall pine and carved: "William Clark December 3rd 1805. By Land from the U. States in 1804 and 1805."

Here are the vast lands explored by Meriwether Lewis and William Clark during their historic expedition from St. Louis to the Pacific Coast. Published in 1814, this map was copied from one that Clark made after his journey and was more accurate than any previous map of the American West. It shows the western mountains as a series of ranges instead of one big range, and includes the nearly correct courses of the Missouri and Snake Rivers.

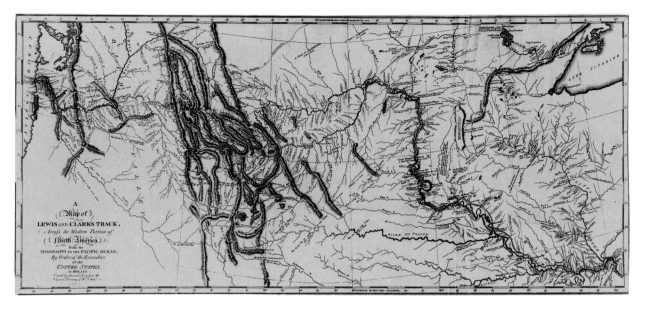

Lewis and Clark didn't find a continuous water route from the East to the Pacific Ocean, but they did survey the land and learn much about the wildlife and people of the country. On the expedition, Native Americans, whom Clark treated with great respect, drew maps for him on hides or on the ground with charcoal or sticks. Clark used this information to make a map based on his journey, which was published in 1814. The map was an instant success, and the two explorers were greatly admired. Other adventuresome explorers could hardly wait to try their skills at filling in the map of America.

Perhaps the most celebrated of the new generation of explorers was the dashing John Charles Frémont, who made three mapping expeditions to the American West. His maps were used by settlers in the 1840s and 1850s.

In the spring of 1843, Frémont set out on his second expedition, during which he explored the Great Salt Lake, marched all the way to California, and erased from maps the Rio Buenaventura, a mythical water route to the West Coast. The dream of a water passage straight to the riches of the Indies, the same hope that had driven Columbus more than three centuries before, was finally put to rest. Along the way, Frémont and his men faced severe winter weather and starvation. One man was so hungry that he stuck his hand in a nest of ants and licked them off.

John Wesley Powell, a Civil War veteran, filled in the last great geographical gap in the map

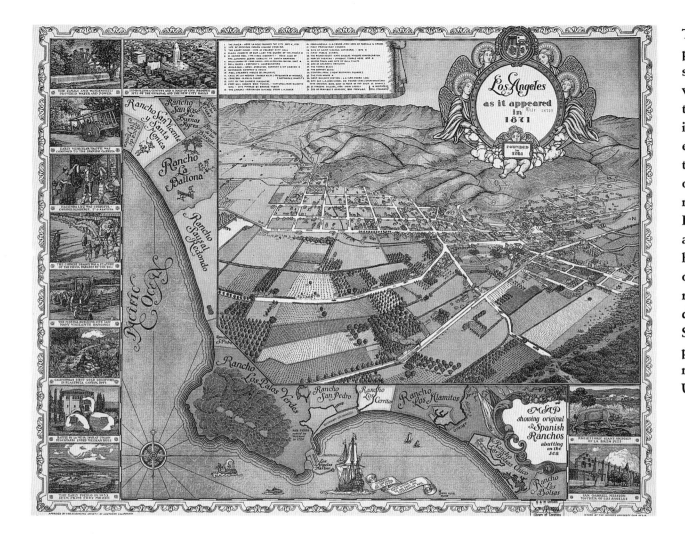

Thousands of panoramic maps, showing bird's-eye views of cities and towns, were published in the nineteenth and early twentieth centuries. This is a copy of an 1871 panoramic map of Los Angeles. Decorating its borders are scenes of city history and pictures of the *ranchos*, or ranches, that thrived during the city's Spanish and Mexican periods, before California became part of the United States in 1848.

of the continental United States. In 1869, Powell and a party of six men (three others had abandoned the expedition when they saw what was ahead) floated a raft down the entire length of the Colorado River, mapping the river from its source in the High Rockies through the Grand Canyon to the Gulf of California. Despite having lost an arm during the Civil War, Powell led the boats through giant rapids and a twenty-foot-high waterfall.

Mapmakers used Powell's survey of the Grand Canyon country and surrounding lands for nearly one hundred years. In 1881, Powell became director of the new U.S. Geological Survey, still the nation's main mapping agency.

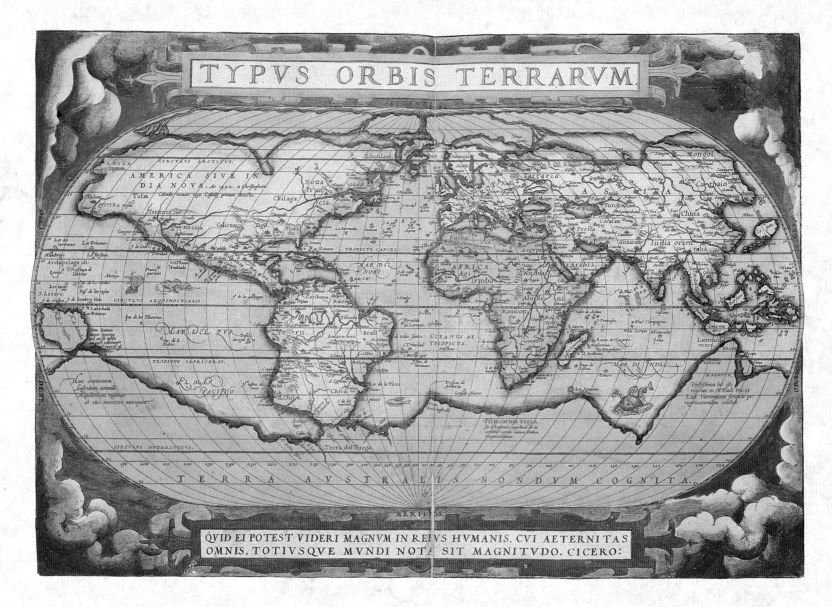

World map by Abraham Ortelius, 1571

CHAPTER 9
THE MYTHICAL CONTINENT THAT REALLY WAS

T*erra Australis Incognita*, or the Unknown Southern Land, sprawls across the bottom of this map by Ortelius, occupying a good portion of the world. But unlike Saint Brendan's paradise or Prester John's kingdom, this mythical continent, which fueled the imaginations of kings, mapmakers, and explorers for more than two thousand years, really does exist. The continent in question may not be the vast, lush land imagined for all those years, but there *is* a continent at the bottom of the world. It's called Antarctica.

Terra Australis Incognita was first put on maps by the ancient Greeks. In the Middle Ages, many Christian mapmakers were troubled by the idea of a fourth continent at the bottom of the world. For one thing, the Bible said that there were only three continents, one for each of Noah's sons. And Europeans did not believe that people could live so far south.

Cosmas, the monk who made the world map in the shape of a trunk, thought the idea of a continent at the bottom, or opposite side, of the earth was ridiculous. He asked: "If two men on opposite sides [of the earth] placed the soles of their feet against each others . . . how could both of them be found standing upright?" Many Christian cartographers erased the Unknown Southern Land from maps for the rest of the Middle Ages.

As part of his search for the Unknown Southern Land in 1768, Captain James Cook mapped all twenty-four hundred miles of the coastline of New Zealand in six months, proving it wasn't part of Australia. This section of his survey shows Duskey Bay. At the bottom are views of the mountainous north and south entrances into the bay.

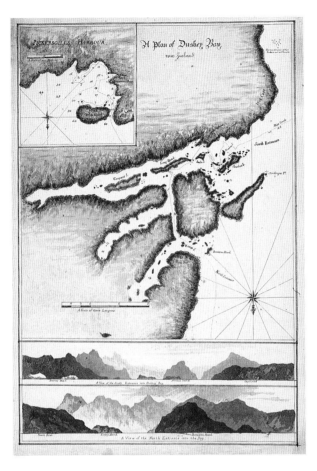

When Ptolemy was rediscovered in the fourteenth century, so was *Terra Australis*, at least in theory. It was usually drawn as a large rectangle at the bottom of the world map, and over the years it grew bigger and bigger. When Ortelius placed the southern continent on the world map of his 1570 atlas, he included such details as rivers and names and gave it the optimistic title *Terra Australis Nondum Cognita*—the Southern Land Not *Yet* Known.

Mapmakers held on to the idea of a great southern continent throughout the next two centuries, even as explorers pushed farther and farther south without finding it. In 1519, while Ferdinand Magellan was navigating the strait named after him at the tip of South America, he saw some land to the south. Magellan's crew thought it was just an island, and they were right. It was the island now called Tierra del Fuego. But Ortelius and other mapmakers included it as the northern tip of *Terra Australis*.

In 1605, the Dutch reached land south of Asia. It wasn't big enough or far enough south to be *Terra Australis*, but it was eventually named Australia after the great southern continent anyway. For more than a hundred years after the Dutch first arrived, mapmakers and explorers were uncertain of Australia's size and shape. Many thought that Australia, New Zealand, and New Guinea were all connected, and perhaps all part of *Terra Australis*. Mapmakers didn't realize that Australia was a separate continent until 1801. Perhaps that's because Australia, which is the world's smallest continent, looks more like a big island.

The Aborigines, the native people of Australia, had a unique sense of place and way of mapping their country. According to Aboriginal legends about the creation of the world, the first

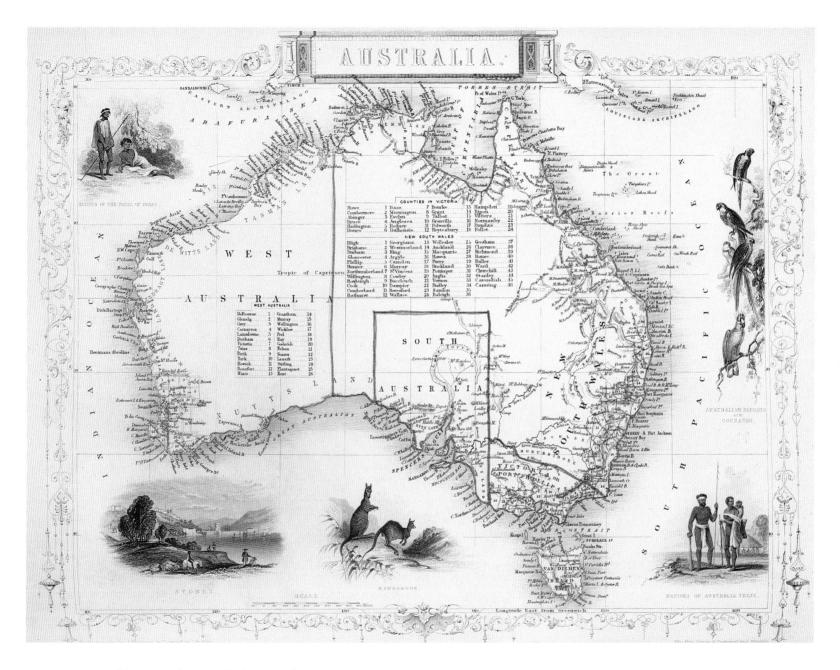

This map of Australia by British engraver John Rapkin was published in 1851 in John Tallis and Company's *Illustrated Atlas and Modern History of the World*. Little was known about the interior of Australia at this time. Around the border are detailed engravings of native people and animals, including parrots, kangaroos, and a cockatoo.

This map shows the actual shape of the continent of Antarctica, a land covered with a thick layer of ice. It was made by putting together twenty-six satellite pictures of different sections of the continent, taken between 1980 and 1987. The numbered areas are the individual satellite images.

beings, the Dreamings, traveled through the country, creating people, plants, and animals. As they walked, they left behind a trail of words and musical notes. If you knew the right song, you could follow a certain path and never lose your way. These invisible paths are known as "Dreaming-tracks" or "Songlines."

Continuing the quest for *Terra Australis*, Captain James Cook set sail from England in 1768. On his first voyage, Cook didn't find the great southern land, but he did carefully chart the entire coast of New Zealand and part of Australia. He proved that Australia and New Zealand were not connected to each other—or to the southern continent. On his second voyage in 1772, he pushed farther south into the Antarctic region. Giant icebergs pitched and rolled around his ships, and his crew suffered from frostbite, but still Cook saw no sign of *Terra Australis*.

A year later he tried again, sailing as far into the frozen wilderness as he possibly could before the bitter cold forced him to turn back for the last time. As it turns out, Cook was within a hundred miles of sighting Antarctica, the real southern

continent, which was smaller and colder than the early mapmakers imagined.

Sailors finally reached Antarctica in 1820. It is the only continent that was truly discovered because nobody lived there when it was found. In fact, it appears nobody has ever lived on the ice-covered continent that is twice the size of western Europe, although researchers have found fossils of plants and trees and, more recently, dinosaurs.

Because Antarctica is so extremely cold (it holds the world's record of 127 degrees below zero), people have been slow to explore and map the continent. We have only known the size and shape of Antarctica for about thirty years, and because it is largely covered by ice, its shape is constantly changing.

Today Antarctica is like a giant science laboratory. No one owns Antarctica, but many countries study its icy depths and extraordinarily clear skies to learn about the atmosphere and the earth's past. The Antarctic Treaty of 1959 guarantees every country's right to use the continent for peaceful purposes.

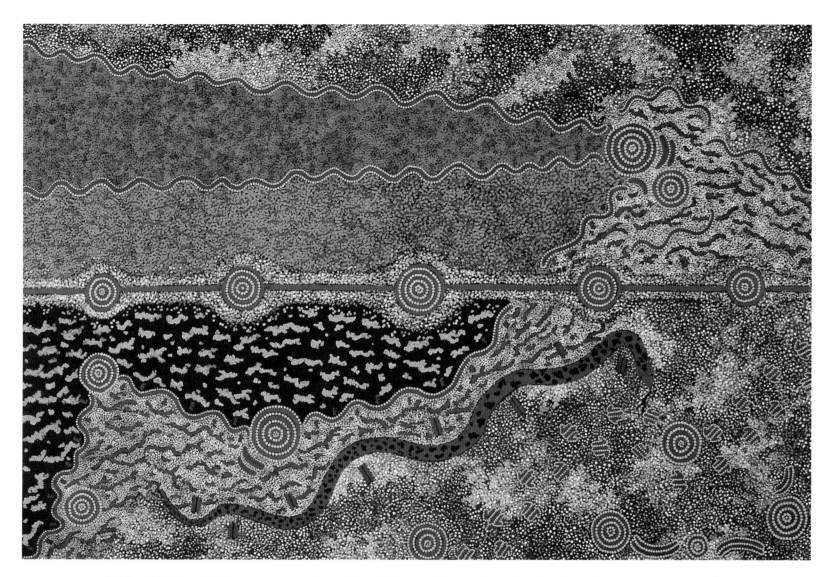

Michael Nelson Tjakamarra, an Australian Aboriginal artist, made this painting called *Five Dreamings* in 1984, with help from his wife Marjorie Napaljarri. In the Aborigines' religion, Dreamings are the first beings that created the people, animals, and plants of the world. While paintings like these are not maps as we know them, they often show real Australian places that are settings for myths about Dreamings.

The red snake in the picture represents the Rainbow Serpent Dreaming at a place called Yilkirdi, near Mount Singleton in Central Australia. The red line across the center is the track of the Flying Ant Dreaming at a place called Yuwinji. The animal tracks in the lower right are the prints of the Two Kangaroo ancestors at Yintarramurru. The wavy lines are Possum ancestor tracks.

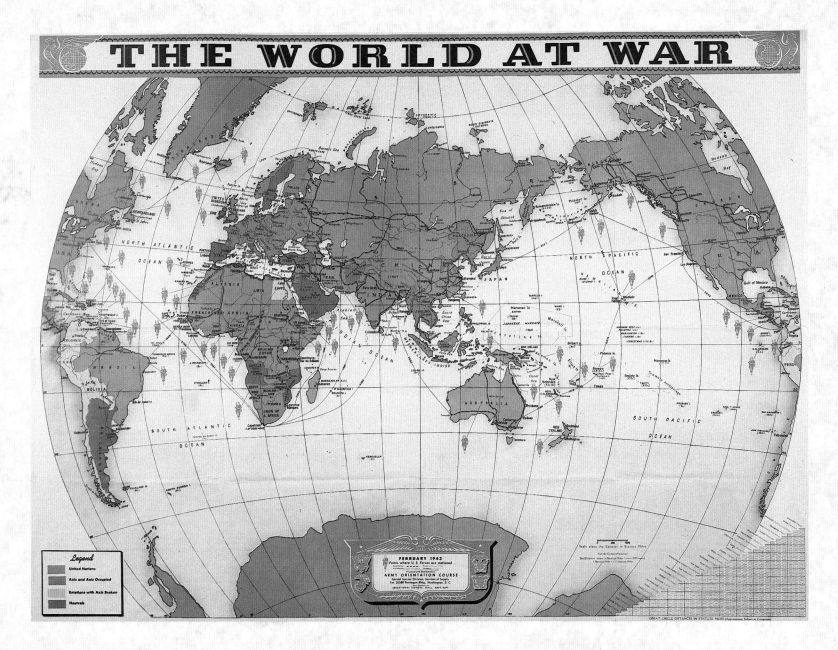

"The World at War," prepared by the Army Special Service Division, February 1943

CHAPTER 10
OUR CHANGING WORLD

Some of the most important features on maps are the lines that separate regions, states, and countries. Sometimes these lines, called *boundary lines*, follow the natural curve of rivers or the physical barrier of a mountain range. Often, though, they are ruler-straight lines, defined by people and governments. Boundaries can unify people and give them an identity as members of a certain state or country, or they can divide people who once lived as a group. These lines, though largely invisible, are so important that people will fight and die for them. Throughout history, the map of the world has changed as wars and peace treaties created new nations and changed the boundaries of others.

This map shows what the world was like in 1943, during the Second World War. Only thirty years before this map was made, on the eve of the First World War, the borders of the nations of Europe looked very different. And less than three years after this map was made, the boundaries of Europe would be redrawn another time.

If you look at the map on the next page of Central Europe in 1914, right before World War I started, you'll see that much of Central and Eastern Europe was under the control of a few large states, including the Austro-Hungarian, German, Ottoman, and Russian empires. There were also some small states—Serbia, Montenegro, Albania, Romania, Bulgaria, and Greece. Some nations that you might know, such as Poland, are missing. Can you find other missing countries?

In 1914, just before World War I, a few large empires controlled much of Central and Eastern Europe.

The various nations in this part of the world feared that one country might get too powerful. Their rivalries led to World War I. Four years later, in 1918, the Austro-Hungarian and German empires were defeated, and the victors met in Paris to redraw the map of Europe. They divided the Austro-Hungarian empire into Austria and Hungary. The states of Montenegro and Serbia were included in the newly formed nation of Yugoslavia. Poland, once an independent kingdom, was re-formed as a nation, and the new nation of Czechoslovakia was created. But simply drawing lines on a map and making a new country does not unify people. The various groups of people included in the new country of Yugoslavia,

for example, continued to consider themselves Serbs, Croats, and Slovenes, not Yugoslavs.

In 1917, a revolution took place in Russia. The old rulers were thrown out and a communist government was established. Five years later, Russia and other republics formed the Union of Soviet Socialist Republics, or Soviet Union.

In 1939, Germany, led by a power-hungry dictator named Adolf Hitler, invaded Poland, and the Second World War began. Britain, France, Russia, and other nations that sided with them, called allies, fought to prevent Germany and its allies from taking control of Europe. The United States joined the war after Japan, which was allied with Germany, bombed America at Pearl Harbor in 1941.

The map at the beginning of the chapter uses different colors to show the alliances, or partnerships, among nations and the movement of troops in February 1943, in the midst of World War II. The pictures of soldiers show the places where American troops were stationed. The Army used this map to teach new soldiers what they would be doing and where they might be going.

The president and military leaders of the United States relied on similar maps to help develop a strategy to win the war. A cloakroom on the ground floor of the White House was turned into a map room. There, people worked around the clock to update maps showing battles and troop positions. Most mornings, President Franklin D. Roosevelt would slowly tour the room, studying maps at close range. The room was so important to the war effort that its existence was kept secret. In the White House today, a map hangs on the wall of what is still known as the Map Room.

In 1945, at the end of World War II, the victors again redrew boundaries in Europe. The Soviet Union took over the nations of Estonia, Latvia, and Lithuania on the Baltic Sea. Germany was divided into East and West Germany, and the Soviet Union took control of the eastern part. Though most boundaries are only lines on a map, East Germany eventually built an actual wall between the two Germanys in the city of Berlin, and East Germans were not allowed to cross it. Several other European nations, including Poland, Czechoslovakia, Hungary, Romania, Yugoslavia, and Bulgaria, also came under the communist form of government.

In the years following World War II, the map of the world continued to change as many countries gained independence from Britain, France, and other nations. Some changed their names in the process. If you compare Africa in the 1943 map with Africa in the modern world map in the center of this book, you'll see several differences. Northern Rhodesia, for instance, gained indepen-

After World War I ended in 1918, many nations, including Poland, Czecho-slovakia, Yugoslavia, Estonia, Latvia, and Lithuania, were carved out of the old empires.

dence and became Zambia. Southern Rhodesia became Zimbabwe, and Tanganyika and Zanzibar united to form Tanzania. See how many other changes you can find.

Mapmakers rely on the United States Board on Geographic Names to keep up with changing names. The board, formed in 1890, the first such agency in the world, votes on name changes and additions every month.

In 1989, events began to take place in Central and Eastern Europe that would change the map of Europe dramatically for the third time since the turn of the century. Communist power began to collapse, and countries held free elections to form non-communist governments.

This 1981 map shows how Europe looked after World War II and after the rise of communist governments in many Eastern European countries. Here Germany has been divided into East and West Germany, and the Soviet Union has regained some of the territory lost by the Russian Empire after World War I.

among Muslim, Serbian, and Croation people in Bosnia-Herzegovina, one of several republics that until recently were part of the former Yugoslavia.

Changes happened so quickly in those few years that sometimes maps were out of date as soon as they were published.

When cartographers at the National Geographic Society were updating their *Atlas of the World*, Soviet rule was breaking down, East and West Germany were considering unification, the Yemen Arab Republic and the People's Republic of Yemen in the Middle East had just merged, and Iraq was threatening to invade Kuwait.

Markie Hunsiker, associate director of the Cartographic Division of the National Geographic Society, thought the society was all set when it finished the sixth edition of the atlas. "We showed a unified Germany and a unified Yemen," she recalls. "It had only been printed for a couple of months, then the Soviet Union broke up, and we had to produce a revised sixth edition. We were really busy."

The National Geographic Society ended up revising their world map five times in eight months to keep up with the changes!

Then, on a cold morning in November, the people of East Germany broke through the Berlin Wall, finally free to cross into West Germany. West Germans threw flowers and shouted *"Herzlich wilkommen"*—a heartfelt welcome!

By December 1991, all fifteen republics of the Soviet Union had voted to become independent nations. The Soviet Union ceased to exist. The changes in this part of the world were exciting, but they brought new problems and, in some places, bloodshed. For example, a terrible war broke out

Today Germany is one nation again. The Soviet Union no longer exists. In its place are the independent nations of Russia, Ukraine, Byelarus, Moldova, and many others. The area that was once Yugoslavia has been divided into Slovenia, Croatia, Bosnia-Herzegovina, Montenegro, Serbia, and Macedonia.

Earth from the *Apollo 11*
spacecraft, July 29, 1969

CHAPTER 11
PICTURES FROM SPACE

Earth, suspended like a ball in space with its swirling bands of blue and white, is a familiar sight. But it was not long ago, December 1968, to be exact, that three astronauts aboard the spacecraft *Apollo 8* first saw the whole world with their own eyes. As astronaut James A. Lovell, Jr., said at the time, "The vast loneliness up here is awe-inspiring, and it makes you realize just what you have back there on Earth. The earth from here is a grand oasis in the big vastness of space." From space the astronauts didn't see a world divided by political and other man-made boundaries. They saw a unified world, divided only by the natural boundaries of land and water.

About a year and a half later, the astronauts on the *Apollo 11* spacecraft viewed the world from ninety-eight thousand nautical miles above Earth, as pictured here. The astronauts could see most of Africa and parts of Europe and Asia. Can you? North America is on the side of the earth that was facing away and is not visible.

Before spacecraft allowed us to get a bird's-eye view of the earth, people came up with some different ideas about the shape and size of the world. Christopher Columbus, for instance, thought the earth was shaped like a pear. And in a way he was right!

In 1958, one of the first space explorers was an unmanned spacecraft named *Vanguard*. By studying *Vanguard*'s orbit, or path, as it traveled around the earth, scientists realized that our planet

In September 1994, the Kliuchevskoi volcano in Kamchatka, Russia, began to erupt, at times spitting gas, vapor, and ash fifty thousand feet into the air. In this radar image, taken from the space shuttle *Endeavour*, the erupting volcano is the blue triangular peak in the center. The bright red area is bare snow. The blue and green lines in the center are mudflows of snow mixed with volcanic ash.

is indeed very slightly pear-shaped. It narrows somewhat at the north and bulges a tiny bit around the center.

New technologies, from satellites to computers, are revealing some very interesting things about the planet we live on.

It all began in the mid-1800s with *aerial photography*, which simply means photographs taken from the air. The first lofty view of the land was taken from a balloon. A Paris photographer who called himself Nadar set up a darkroom in the basket of a balloon and floated above a village to take photographs.

Today, almost all original maps are made using some method of aerial photography. Rather than taking measurements on the ground, pilots fly airplanes in a series of straight lines while cameras on board take photographs of the land and its features.

Photographs of the earth's surface are also taken from *satellites*, small man-made objects that orbit the planet four hundred to six hundred miles high. By sensing light that is not visible to the human eye, satellites allow us to view things that we can't "see" in the normal way. Light is the source of all color. Light travels in waves, and different wavelengths of light appear to us as different colors. When the sun's white light, which is a mixture of all colors, shines on the ocean, the water absorbs most of the wavelengths. But it reflects the wavelengths that appear blue to us, so we see a blue ocean.

The colors of the rainbow that we see, ranging from red to violet, are called a spectrum. Beyond the ends of this spectrum are colors we can't see—for example, *infrared*, meaning below red. Infrared and other invisible light can be seen by special cameras and sensors, the eyes of a satellite. The sensors scan the earth below and measure the light it reflects. The measurements are sent to the ground, where computers turn them into pictures. This gives scientists a new way to see and understand the world. Leaves of healthy, growing plants, for instance, reflect a high level of infrared wavelengths and appear red on special film. Sick or dead plants appear light red or even blue. An infrared photograph of a forest can quickly show if it is healthy or not.

This infrared photo of the Missouri and Mississippi Rivers was taken from a NASA aircraft on July 29, 1993, during heavy flooding. Urban areas appear as white or blue, plant life as red, and the flooded river as blue green. The normal channel of the Missouri River is visible between the two red lines winding upward from left center. The white dots in the water are homes and other buildings caught in the flood.

Satellites can take pictures through clouds, which allowed cartographers in the 1970s to map the Amazon Basin of Brazil for the first time in spite of its thick forests and constant cloud cover. Satellite images showed the correct locations of streams, mountain ranges, and forests, and even revealed hills and a one-hundred-mile-long river that were previously unknown. Now satellite images show how quickly the Amazon rain forest is being cut down.

This map, which was generated by a computer, shows the places in the continental United States most likely to experience earthquakes. The higher the peaks are, the greater the earthquake risk. The purple peaks in southern California are the areas of highest risk. To make this map, a scientist fed the computer information about past earthquakes.

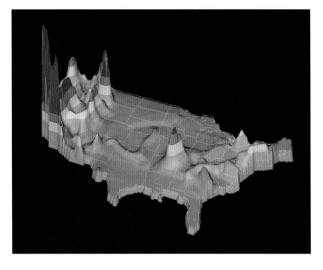

Satellite images are a type of *remote sensing*, which means learning about something without touching it. When you hold your hands near a fire to feel how hot it is, you are using remote sensing. Photography is a common type of remote sensing. Other kinds of remote sensing used by mapmakers include sonar (short for Sound Navigation and Ranging), radar, and seismic, or earthquake, measurements. Using remote sensing, cartographers have been able to map areas previously thought unmappable, such as the ocean floor, the earth's interior, and the land below the polar ice caps.

Geographical information gathered using aerial or satellite photography and other types of remote sensing is stored in computers. Mapmakers use computers, with the stored information, to make highly accurate maps in a matter of

hours. Once a map is displayed on a computer screen, cartographers can quickly make corrections or additions, change the projection, or zoom in on a small section of the map. Cartographers can also combine the geographical information with other sets of facts contained in the computer, such as population or earthquake records. Police investigators, for example, can combine a map of a city with police records to analyze crime patterns and help solve cases. In Salt Lake City, Utah, which has an earthquake fault running through it, the U.S. Geological Survey combined maps of roads and fire stations with earthquake information to see how quickly fire and rescue squads could reach different parts of the city in case of an earthquake.

In the future, you may be able to avoid traffic jams with the help of a computer on your car dashboard. The computer could link a map of your route with traffic information to tell you the quickest way home.

What you have seen in this book is a small sampling of the wide world of maps. Millions of maps, atlases, and globes from all time periods and from every corner of the world are waiting for you to explore. There are many different types of maps, other than world maps, that you can use for different purposes. Some maps show roads and tourist sites to help you plan a trip. *Topographic*

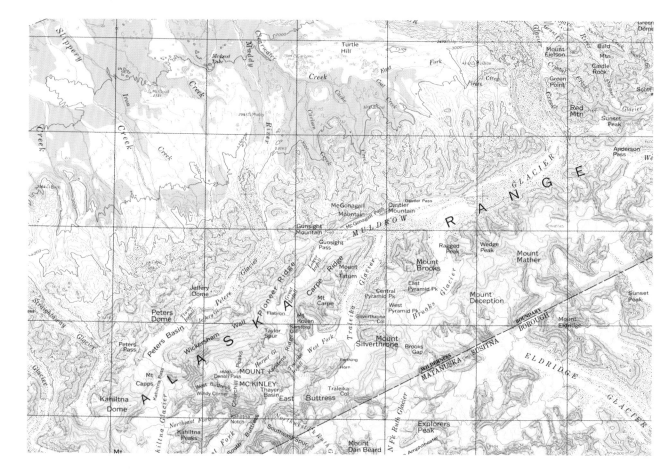

maps show the natural and man-made features on the surface of the earth in great detail. These maps include the *elevations*—the distances up and down—of mountains and valleys and are especially useful to hikers. Sailors use special maps called *marine* or *nautical charts* that show coastlines, harbors, lighthouses, and underwater rocks that could tear holes in the bottoms of boats.

The next time you pick up a map, whether new or old, practical or decorative, ask yourself:

Who made this map and why? What is its purpose? What are the special features of this map? Then look closely at the details to see what else you can learn. What do the illustrations tell you about the people of the area? How does the projection affect the shapes and sizes of the continents? Has the world changed since this map was made?

Follow maps closely, and they will do more than help you find your way—they will lead you to a better understanding of the world.

For my family

ACKNOWLEDGMENTS

With appreciation to Richard W. Stephenson, retired specialist in American cartographic history, Library of Congress, Geography and Map Division, for his expertise and guidance, and a special thanks to Nancy Kober for her many hours spent in search of the perfect maps.

Published by Thomasson-Grant & Lickle
Designed by Alexandra Littlehales
     and Lisa Lytton-Smith
Edited by Nancy Kober and Deborah Sussman

Copyright © 1996 Lickle Publishing
Text © 1995 Yvette La Pierre

Printed and bound in Hong Kong.

Library of Congress Cataloging-in-Publication Data

La Pierre, Yvette.
     Mapping a changing world / by Yvette La Pierre ; edited by Nancy Kober.
          p. cm.
     Summary: Traces the history of maps, from the oldest known map etched on a clay tablet to a radar image from the space shuttle, and discusses how they have evolved with changes in knowledge, science, culture, and tools.
     ISBN 0-9650308-4-9 (hardcover)
     1. Cartography--Juvenile literature. [1. Cartography. 2. Maps.] I. Kober, Nancy. II. Title.
GA105.6.L3 1995
526--dc20   95-35241
                                                          CIP
                                                          AC

ILLUSTRATION CREDITS: Courtesy of the Library of Congress, Geography and Map Division: front cover and pages 2, 7, 8, 11, 15, 16, 25, 28, 50, 53, 56, 59, 61, 62, 65. National Aeronautics and Space Administration: back cover and pages 10, 74, 76, 77. National Maritime Museum, London: page 4. Copyright British Museum: pages 12, 48. The Walters Art Gallery, Baltimore: page 14. American Numismatic Society: page 21. By permission of the British Library: page 22 (Add MS 28681 fol. 9), page 31 (Add 16356), page 32 (Maps 63055 (2)), page 37 (Royal 14 CVII fols. 2v & 3), page 39 (Add MS 5415A fols. 15v-16), page 55 (9 Tab 8 (103)), page 58 (K. Top CXII 35), page 64 (Add MS 15500 no. 3). Florence, Biblioteca Medicea Laurenziana with permission of the Ministero per i Beni Culturali e Ambientali: page 24. The Tracy W. McGregor Library, Special Collections Department, University of Virginia Library: pages 26, 27, 47, 49, 54, 60. Jean-Claude Ciancimino: page 33. Bibliothèque Nationale de France, Paris: page 34. By permission of the Bodleian Library, Oxford: page 36 (MS POCOCKE 375 fols. 3v/4r), page 46 (MS Arch. Selden. A. 1, fol. 2r). Central Intelligence Agency: pages 40, 70, 71, 72, 73. American Congress on Surveying and Mapping: pages 42, 43. Courtesy of the James Ford Bell Library, University of Minnesota: page 44. U.S. Geological Survey: pages 66, 79. Aboriginal Artists Agency: page 67. National Archives and Records Administration: page 68. Melvin L. Prueitt, Los Alamos National Laboratory: page 78.

Any inquiries should be directed to:
Thomasson-Grant & Lickle
106 South Street
Charlottesville, VA 22902-5039
(804) 977-1780